THE

"O"

FACTOR

Relationship Principles for Women

Dr. Sybil B. Pentsil

The "O" Factor

Copyright ©2018 Dr. Sybil Pentsil

Dr. Sybil Pentsil
Baltimore, Maryland

Publisher:
Elite Online Publishing
63 East 11400 South #230
Sandy, UT 84070
www.EliteOnlinePublishing.com

ISBN-13: 978-1983940347
ISBN-10: 1983940348

DEDICATION

To all the "O" Factor women in my life:

You have been my help and strength

Your example and drive have kept me going

Your shoulders have been my solace during the tough times

Your arms have held me and your hands have pushed me

It is because of you that I don't quit

You are my mothers, daughters, sisters and friends

You know who you are

I love you so much

This one is for you!

ACKNOWLEDGMENTS

Vanessa Addison – you used to refer to me as your mother-daughter-sister-friend. For years the concept resonated with me; that one woman could be so many different things to another. Thank you Vanessa! You were the seed of this book and I am so grateful.

My mother in the Lord Martha Kure - you never cease to amaze me with your acceptance, love, prayers, and drive to serve the Lord. I am eternally grateful for your life. You have the "O" Factor! I love and appreciate you and Daddy Kure so much!

Sharon Adefarasin – you are so many things to me but I especially love that I have a friend in you! Thanks for your encouragement and ideas as I worked on this project.

Michelle McKinney Hammond - what an amazing sister and friend I found in you! I love you!

My spiritual son and daughter Cy and Edwina Forh – I couldn't have done this without your love, encouragement, support and hard work. You are simply the best! My life is eternally blessed because you are in it.

Fiifi, Jeremy, Jason, and Jesse – my loves, my life, my heart itself!

TABLE OF CONTENTS

FOREWORD

A lot has been said about women in the Bible. Just when you think it has all been said a different perspective emerges. One that is refreshing, intuitive and relevant to where we are today. Sybil Pentsil has thoughtfully looked at all the aspects and expressions of who we are as women and offers clear principles for us to live our God intended best life. She takes a look at the good, the bad and the ugly, who we can be and who we shouldn't be in a down to earth way that challenges us to be authentic in our approach to life and others we encounter. The *"O" Factor* will empower you to live in a manner that positively impacts those around you and leaves a lasting legacy for generations to come.

Michelle McKinney Hammond

Bestselling author of The Power Of Being A Woman

INTRODUCTION

The "O" Factor

Relationship Principles for Women

The Sister Hat - Wisdom

The Worker Hat - Balance

The Daughter Hat - Practice

The Friend Hat – Sense

The Wife Hat - Endurance

The Rival Hat - Perspective

The Mistress Hat - Strength

The Servant Hat – Self-Worth

The Lover Hat - Timing

The Mother Hat - Vision

The Rejected Hat - Purpose

The Beloved Hat - Boundaries

1

2

CHAPTER ONE

THE SISTER HAT

How do I relate to my sisters by birth? What kinds of things did we do as children? In what ways does she drive me crazy? What holds us together as sisters? Which of my friends do I relate to as a sister?

Obaasima Principle: WISDOM

The key to wearing the sister hat well is to know who you are, know who your siblings are, have healthy expectations of them and have healthy expectations of yourself!

1. Create proper and realistic boundaries around your role as a sister.

2. Know who you are to each of your siblings.

3. Don't take on more than you should.

4. Love your siblings whether they deserve it or not.

5. Loving them doesn't mean making crazy sacrifices you shouldn't make.

6. Your siblings are different; know how to relate to each one.

7. Don't allow guilt to make you change your standards.

There is at least one thing in life that none of us can choose: we can't choose the families into which we are born. You cannot select your natural sister. She just appears in your life. You may love her or hate her. You could be good friends or maybe you just tolerate one another. You may be alike or extremely different. No matter how you feel about her, she is your sister and there is absolutely nothing you can do about it. Sisterhood is not situation-dependent or impacted by circumstances. It is a permanent relationship! Hardship, triumph or joy may come, but you remain sisters regardless of the season. As a child, I remember being told many times to speak and act in a particular way towards my sisters for no other reason than that they were my sisters. I find myself teaching this same principle to my sons. Years ago my oldest son had only one responsibility. It was to protect his little brother. That was his job. Yes, we taught him to take care of his toys and obey the adults around him, but his job at all times was to protect his brother. This was not always an easy task for him, because his little brother was a boisterous and strong-willed toddler! That little boy would kick, whine and scream, but his older brother was still responsible for him. The principle we were trying to teach our sons was that they must embrace their brotherhood, and learn to love each other even when they felt it wasn't deserved. The bond of brotherhood was to tie them together at all times and compel at least one of them to do what is right, and hopefully help draw both of them into a relationship of peace and love. The same is true for sisterhood. The bond of sisterhood must tie sisters together at all times and compel at least one of us to do what is right and draw both of us into a relationship of peace and love. If we're going to have to deal with someone forever, then we need to figure out how to do it well, don't we? If I have to love my sister forever, then I need to figure out how to love her.

Love is multidimensional but it is rooted in respect. It is a decision. It is a code of conduct that maintains our love for each other as sisters. The romantic love (*eros*) between a husband and wife is different from the protective love (*storge*) between mother and child, and is different from the happy love (*phileo*) between friends and is still different from the unselfish love (*agape*) that compelled Jesus to go to the cross for us. The love we have between us as sisters is the *storge* kind of love. It is the love of a comfortable relationship; a natural affection and sense of belonging in a relationship between siblings or parents and children. However, just as a mother can indeed forget her child (Isaiah 49:15), this love can change. The comfortable *storge* love between sisters can get real uncomfortable when one of us decides to go out there and do something crazy! And sometimes the crazy one isn't just the sister who did something wrong. The other sister can get pretty crazy with how she responds, can't she? She can get crazy by excusing the behavior, or funding the behavior, or taking on more than what she should. Isn't that something? We assume the bond of sisterhood and its *storge* love compel us to carry each other at all times and in all circumstances but that's not true. The key to loving one another as sisters is to love with wisdom, not with emotion!

When you love someone, you tolerate more from that person than you do from a stranger. Forgiveness is rooted in love. Haven't you heard yourself making excuses for people you love? "She's just a baby!" or "He is becoming a Christian!" We forgive and make excuses for their mistakes and we forgive our own inadequacies. You know the line we use, right? It's the infamous "God knows my heart!" Yes, yes, yes! We do love ourselves that much! On the flip side of things, we also expect more from the people we love, and that is why we get so hurt when problems arise or when they do things we don't expect. Yes, she might get away with the 'little sins' easily, but those major betrayals tend to hit so much harder when it comes from a loved one. This can be part of the nature of the relationship between sisters: We forgive and excuse some things, but can become very broken by other issues. This kind of up-and-down love is not healthy. Sisters must learn how to navigate these tendencies with wisdom, tempering forgiveness and hurt with accountability and continued love and acceptance.

Being sisters doesn't mean you have to be best friends. There are sisters who are good friends with each other, and others who are more like acquaintances. There are sisters who share more of a mother-daughter type of relationship because of the age difference. And then there are sisters who really dislike each other! These variations in relationship are illustrated quite well in many families.

There is no one uniform standard for how we will relate to each other as sisters. Unfortunately sometimes we think that loving our sisters means we must be best friends. We assume that our sisters are trustworthy. We give our sisters access to things they shouldn't have access to. And then there is the other end of the spectrum where we think that being best friends is out of the question because we simply can't stand each other. Come on sisters, we can do much better than that! How we manifest our love for one another will differ based on our history and experiences with each other. Did you catch that? **There is no standard love for all sisters.** The manifestation of our love will be different. It must be different. Based on our personalities, what has happened between us, and the seasons of life we find ourselves in, how we love one sister must be different from how we love the other! It takes wisdom to love our sisters effectively. It takes wisdom to know when to overlook an offense and when to demand an apology. It takes wisdom to know how to demand an apology in a loving and meaningful way. It takes wisdom to know when to intervene and when to withhold help. Loving a sister effectively is all about wisdom. That wisdom will guide us when our sisters reject us because we don't help them the way they want. That wisdom will direct us to love our sisters even when they are kicking at us. That wisdom will teach us how to rise above each troubling circumstance. That wisdom will compel us to show love even when it isn't deserved. That wisdom will show us how to love.

When David ran away from Saul and escaped to the cave of

Adullam, the Bible says that all kinds of discontented people surrounded him. Can you imagine that? Some of them didn't know too much about God; all they knew was that David had killed Goliath. Others knew God and perceived that they needed to follow David. Some may have come in because they were tired of Saul's regime and wanted to be part of something new. Unfortunately, the Bible does not say much about what happened while they were living in that cave, but when they came out to face Saul, they came out as a strong army of fighting men with one goal: to follow David and protect him. I believe that the strength of the army was the result of each of them coming to a place of recognizing their uniform goal. That is what caused them to put aside their discontentment and pursue their goal. Christians have a world of adopted relatives. We are bound by our family name (Christ), and our bloodline, which is the blood of Jesus. Love them or hate them, all those other Christians become your family. Jesus himself referred to us as his sisters, thus, the most basic level of relationship between unrelated Christian women is sisterhood. However, just like David's cave, the church is never going to be a uniform group of people who always say and do things correctly, where offenses never occur and life is just peachy. On the contrary, church tends to be a place of incredible character diversity. People have different way of expressing themselves, different mentalities, diverse financial strains and gains, and different experiences in life. We encounter different types of women. Some of us come from broken homes. Others have had wonderful families. Some have difficult relationships with their husbands, others don't have a husband but want one, yet others have a wonderful marriage relationship, and another group are not married and don't want a husband. Some are secure in their Christian walk, others are still searching. Some have been Christians for decades while others just accepted Christ into their hearts. Some of us are like my older son who had to make the sacrifice for the sake of the relationship. Some of us are like my younger son was - always kicking, whining and screaming our way through. There will never be a time when we are all exactly the same. We will always be different, but we will always be sisters. Until we accept our common tie as sisters and make those needed sacrifices for the sake of our relationship, we cannot be a strong, united army like David's men were.

Remember how my mother made my sisters and I do things simply because we were sisters? That same principle applies to how we relate to our natural and adopted sisters. Although there is no defined nature of the sisterhood relationship, there are certain basic principles we must apply. Mutual respect, love and forgiveness must be the motive behind everything we do as sisters. I know we would all like to believe that we are practicing these principles all the time but we are not. Whenever there is backbiting, anger, offense and hurt between sisters, it is because somebody failed to act out of respect, love and forgiveness, and another person failed to respond out of respect, love and forgiveness. What does it mean to respect one another? Webster's dictionary defines it in the following ways:

a. To feel or show honor or esteem for; hold in high regard

b. To consider or treat with deference or dutiful regard

c. To show consideration for; avoid intruding upon or interfering with

d. To concern; relate to

Synonyms. To esteem, honor, regard, deference;

1. [To esteem] — To regard, value, look up to; see admire

2. [To treat with consideration] — To heed, appreciate, consider, note, recognize, defer to, show consideration for, show regard for, do honor to, be kind to, show courtesy to, spare, take into account, attend, uphold, refrain from intruding upon.

Is this how we relate to our sisters? I wish I could say that it's precisely what I do, but I struggle with it too! But regardless of the struggles we face, this is the right thing to do.

Even if your sister is not worthy of admiration, and your feelings towards her are not pleasant, you need to listen to what the Holy Spirit says about her. For every sister who has ever ticked me off, the Holy Spirit still had something great to say about her! He would remind me that she too was a child of God, a daughter of the King, and one whom God loves dearly. And I would say, "What??? Are you sure???" But soon I would realize that that my frustration didn't change God's love for her! Then I would quickly get off my high horse and choose to love my sister. Until we can set aside our own pride and self-elevation and begin to see a sister the way God sees her, we won't be able to put our feelings aside and show her respect as a sister. Paul told the Corinthians that he does not regard anyone from a human point of view. We need to see one another through the eyes of the Spirit and not just based on the flesh. That means we see each other as God sees us. And God doesn't see us as perfect. Far from it! He knows our hearts, He sees our faults, He knows just how ugly we can get, and He still sees a child He's going to love. That's what it means to see one another through the eyes of the Spirit. When we recognize that our sisters are princesses in the court of our God just as we are, we will hold one another in higher regard than we usually do.

So how do we become experts at loving our sisters? Wisdom. That is the "O" Factor Principle for women who want to wear the sister hat well. Be wise as a sister. Recognize your bond as sisters, but don't take your relationship for granted. Refuse to be so angry with each other that you fail to see that God made you sisters for a reason. And don't cover up for each other so well that you are sponsoring your own sister's downfall. Apply wisdom in your relationship with your sisters. What seems to make sense in the natural might not be the right thing to do. The wise path is not always the one that will make everyone happy. In fact, the wise path can still get you in a whole lot of trouble with your sister! Wisdom shows us the right thing to do at various points in time. How cool is that? How important too, because your sister isn't going anywhere! You can't 'unfriend' her! And that sister who 'unfriended' you? She needs you more than you know. You need wisdom to love her even though she doesn't want your love. By wisdom you can woo her back into relationship.

The book of James teaches us to ask God for wisdom if we want it. Are you dealing with a tough situation with your sister? Ask God for wisdom. Are there aspects of your relationship that need growth? Ask God for wisdom. Are things great between you? Ask God for wisdom. Are you about to make a major sacrifice for your sister but you aren't sure it's the right thing to do? Ask God for wisdom. Are you at your wits' end? Stop for a minute right now and ask God to show the right way to go. If you're going to rock the sister hat, you will need some wisdom.

Hats off to these sisters!

OUR EXAMPLE - Mary & Martha

These sisters were very different in character. In all portions of the Bible where Martha is described she is busy: cooking, making preparations, running to meet Jesus. Mary on the other hand, is always laid back and relaxed: sitting and listening to Jesus, staying behind and waiting for Jesus to come unlike Martha who ran to him. There is one difficult situation between them that is described in the gospels. Jesus had come over for a visit and Mary sat at his feet listening to him, while Martha did all the cooking and preparations. After a while, Martha got tired of doing all the work, so she complained to Jesus, and asked him to tell her sister to get up and help her. Jesus responded in Mary's favor, and told Martha that Mary had chosen the better portion. Martha's reaction to this rebuke is not recorded. I don't know if she was satisfied with Jesus' wisdom on the matter but there is no record of tension between these two sisters after Jesus' response. Jesus' closeness to them and their brother Lazarus suggests that Jesus enjoyed their company. Can you imagine that? Jesus just liked to hang out with them and relax! I don't think Jesus would specifically go to a place of chaos and strife for no other reason but to relax. Yes, there were times when he rested in the midst of stormy situations, but he didn't seek out a stormy situation just for a nap. But this family? He sought them out and would visit them specifically for rest and relaxation. For Jesus to seek out this family, I believe these sisters (and their brother too) had a wonderful relationship. I believe they were sisters who guarded their relationship with wisdom. They argued, they laughed, and they disagreed but in the midst of it all, they remained sisters. What a wonderful relationship! What a great example of sisterhood!

Watch out for these sisters

OUR CAUTION - Lean and Rachel

This is one of those relationships where the differences between the sisters are glaring: Leah is described as having weak eyes but Rachel is described as beautiful. Leah got pregnant quickly but Rachel was barren for years. Leah was tolerated by Jacob, but Rachel was loved and desired by him. Leah needed a trick to get Jacob to marry her, but he willingly and eagerly married Rachel Jacob. Leah was donated by her father but Rachel was bought with 14 years of hard labor. I am surprised that these women did not kill each other! These sisters had to share the same husband in the midst of all these glaring differences. They even came up with their own well-planned out peace treaties. At another point in their history, Leah sold a bowl of food to her sister for a night with Jacob. Makes you wonder if Leah had to work extra hard to get Jacob to be with her. Rachel consented to this plan and got her food. Very little is said about how these sisters actually related to one another. Their story simply highlights their glaring differences in the midst of their bond as sisters. That should teach us a thing or two about keeping the bond even when 'she's not like me' or 'she has what I want'. If God expects us to love our enemies, then He certainly expects more from us towards our sisters even if we are different! Somehow Leah and Rachel found a way to get along, but they walked a fine line. Leah and Rachel are a caution to us because sometimes one or both of them did indeed cross the line. Fortunately for them, God was gracious and allowed them to birth the twelve tribes of Israel.

These women wore the sister hat in all the wrong ways

OUR WARNING – Lot's Daughters

Think about these girls the next time you have an opportunity to impact your sister's life. The older sister decided that having a child was more important than how she got the child. She just had to have a child but there were no men around. Wait a minute. There was one man available – their Dad. He was lurking around doing nothing but getting old. Maybe he could be the father of her child. But he would never agree to such a plan. That's when she had what she thought was a marvelous idea. She instigated her sister into joining her to get Dad drunk and then sleep with him so they could have children and preserve their family name. Their little scheme worked. Dad got drunk, and slept with both of them and both girls became pregnant. The products of these acts were Moab and Ben-Ammi, the fathers of the Moabites and the Ammonites, two nations that tormented Israel for many, many years. You don't need me to tell you that this instigation was not an act of wisdom! As sisters, we have the power to influence one another. We must use that influence to spur one another on towards righteousness and the pursuit of what is best for our lives. How many times do we draw our very own sisters into wrong behaviors and beliefs that promote evil instead of good? We might draw others by our words, and others are drawn by our actions. Women who serve in any leadership capacity must be particularly weary of this. The way you respond to authority in your life affects how younger sisters will respond to authority. How you relate to your spouse can impact what your sister does. What you say to your sister can have great impact on her choices. Learn from Lot's girls' mistakes. Use wisdom. Impact your sisters for good and not for evil.

These sisters had the "O" factor!

They wore the sister hat with WISDOM!

OUR GOAL - Mahlah, Noah, Hoglah, Milcah, and Tirzah.

These wonderful sisters were the daughters of Zelophahad. Zelophahad was not a rebellious man, but he died en route to Canaan. In their custom, there was no provision for a man who died without a son. So these sisters arrived in the Promised Land without a father or a brother. By custom when it was time to divide the land they would get nothing. Can you imagine that? Taking a long trip, hearing about the promises of God, moving into a new territory and then realizing that you would get nothing! That got these sisters worried. Like Lot's girls, they had a legitimate concern about their future. But unlike Lot's girls, they handled the matter the right way.

First of all, all five sisters agreed on a course of action. That alone is a miracle! How do five girls with different personalities and different opinions agree on a plan of action? I don't know how they did it, but these sisters did! The plan was to go to Moses, their leader, and appeal the custom. Rather than break custom like Lot's girls did, they decided to legally alter the custom so they could obtain their inheritance the right way. Now that is wisdom! So they went to Moses, and Moses went to God and God agreed with the sisters! The result of their actions was the institution of a law requiring inheritance to be left to daughters if there was no son to carry the family name. Amazing! These sisters stood together and had an impact for good that would bless them and many daughters after them. They are our heroines because they demonstrate the life-changing level of relationship that sisters must have, where our bond of sisterhood positively changes our destiny, and the destiny of those around us. Bravo sisters!

CHAPTER TWO

THE WORKER HAT

What is work? How do I make choices? Do I think carefully before making purchases? What role does work play in my life? Do my day-to-day activities reflect an investment into the ultimate goals for my life? What am I working for? Who am I working for?

Obaasima Principle: BALANCE

The key to wearing the worker hat well is to make all your other hats work together! Without balance you will be miserable at work and everywhere else.

1. Be in the right career, in the right position, and with the right schedule.

2. If you are going to work, then be prepared to work hard.

3. Get this: you have to work hard at work and everywhere else!

4. Unless work is #1 for you, don't sacrifice your #1 for the sake of work.

5. Know when the money isn't worth it.

6. Be flexible. Career changes are not suicide.

7. Do what you love, and be sure to love what you do!

A Woman's Workplace

We usually think of our places of employment when we consider the word 'work' but I'd like to challenge that point of view. There are many things we do that require some work, a lot of work in some cases. For example the efforts we put into our relationships take a whole lot of energy. In this chapter I would like us to focus on all the things that make us tired at the end of the day: the career, housework, home schooling, child care and training, volunteer activities, and church commitments are all work and for a woman it is exhausting! Why does our work encompass so much and yet it seems like the guys are chilling? It's because for a woman, her workplace is not just her job; her entire life is her workplace! We approach everything with strength, diligence and excellence. We work hard at everything and while that's a strength, it is also a glaring weakness when we choose to work at the wrong thing. In the rest of this chapter, I shall refer to 'work' as a collective word encompassing the categories just listed, and the word 'career' shall refer to the things we do to generate income. In this chapter, we shall examine various perspectives on work and how to tie all the roles we play into one job. Later on in The "O" Factor, we will tackle attitudes about working but for now let's focus on the Obaasima Principle for worker-bee ladies like you and I: Balance!

Nobody wants to sit on a three-legged chair because it's much easier to sit on a chair that is itself comfortably balanced on 4 nice strong legs. If you are going to rock the worker hat, you need to be balanced. You need to be balanced as an individual wearing multiple hats or you are going to get knocked off by the pressures of everything you are trying to do. I conceptualize balance as a chair with these 4 nice strong legs: reason, choices, career, and time.

1. **Reason** – Why are you doing all the things you are doing? If you don't have good reasons, you will spend a whole lot of time working but not feel fulfilled. Good reason keeps our minds stable when we are pulled in a million directions. Good reason gives us hope when we want to quit. Good reason keeps us grounded and focused in the midst of all the things we are trying to accomplish. We all have different seasons and phases of life, each with its own unique purpose and plan. Ask yourself the following questions:

- Do I enjoy work?

- Do I want to work outside my home?

- What are the things I enjoy doing the most?

- What am I good at?

- Am I the kind of person who needs some hours outside the house each day?

- Do I want to have children? If so, at what stages in my life?

- Am I comfortable leaving my children with a babysitter?

21

Daycare? Public School? Private School?

- What are my beliefs about a woman having a career?

- What are my beliefs about a mother having a career?

- Do I want to get married?

- Do I want to have a good marriage, an okay marriage or just a marriage?

- How much money do I need? How much money do I want?

- What price am I willing to pay for the money I want?

- Do I enjoy working with people? Pets? Objects? Theories?

- What do I want to accomplish with this career?

- Would I be okay if I never had children?

- What are my thoughts about birth control?

- If I needed to give up my career for my family, would I be comfortable?

- What is important to me right now? List the order of importance.

- Does my life right now reflect those priorities?

- What major goals do I want to accomplish in life?

- Is my life right now preparing me for these goals?

I know, you're thinking these are a lot of questions. But if you don't understand yourself and your unique desires and needs during the different seasons of your life, you will do things for the wrong reasons and it will leave you imbalanced. Once you have answered these questions, re-evaluate your reasons for doing what you do and you will find that some things on your to-do list have just got to go!

2. Choices - We cannot make wise choices until we understand what we want or need for each stage of our lives, and indeed our desires and needs may change. So if you read ahead and didn't answer the questions above, go back and answer them. You might have a good reason, but it doesn't make it a wise choice. When we don't take the time to examine ourselves first, we end up running strings of little choice experiments. Then we end up getting into trouble, then we spend time fixing up after ourselves, miss the time we should have been investing into our future, and then it turns into a vicious cycle we can't ever seem to get out of. Our choices can affect our lives forever. Our choice of a spouse, our choice of when to have children, our choice of a career, our choice of how much time to put into our careers, our choice of when to spend money, our choice of how to train our children, our choice of extracurricular activities, our choice of church activities. All these issues are part and parcel of our lives as women, and we must make choices that will put us on a path for success, not pain. But the choices start with understanding what we want. Then we must decide how important those 'wants' are to us. How many of us want to get out of debt, but still keep using those credit cards to buy things we don't need? We do that because even though we know what we want, it isn't really top on our priority list. And where does God fit into all these priorities? How valuable and true is the Bible to you? Does God's law regarding these choices do anything for you at all? I put it this way because frankly, so many of us are just so callous to the Word of God. God's mandates to us about career, sex, marriage, motherhood and family do not matter to a whole lot of us. And we expect to live fulfilled lives as women? It will not happen for the 'Christian' woman who chooses to live outside the Word of God. So there's the desire, the priority, the Word, and then comes the choice. This is not necessarily in order of importance. In fact, sometimes our desires are so wild and crazy that they overcome everything else in us. Sometimes it is best to start with what the Word says first, so we can kill a lot of ungodly desires even before they start. This requires careful and clear understanding of what the Bible says about each of our work choices. And for those issues that are not addressed directly by the Bible, (like whether to work for the bank or for city hall, whether to marry Christian Joe or Christian Mo, whether to have a child in the first year of marriage or in the tenth) prayer and godly counsel cannot be underestimated.

3. Career - Now, let's get over one big stumbling block right now. There is nothing wrong with a woman choosing to work outside the home. There are numerous women in the Bible who had careers and some of them were married with children.

- Priscilla was a tentmaker

- Dorcas was a seamstress

- Joanna and Susanna were full time ministers who traveled with Jesus

- Deborah was a judge

- The virtuous wife sought after for Solomon would be a homemaker, business woman, mother and well praised wife

So there is nothing evil about being a career woman. But there are various mistakes that we make concerning our careers that turns them into an unnecessary evil and gives the devil foothold to ruin our lives. First of all, what is the purpose of our careers? It is not a means to get money to do what we want. We get that warped mentality from our teenage years when we got supermarket jobs so we could buy all the things our parents wouldn't buy for us. And then there are those of us who use our jobs as a little security blanket so we can always take care of ourselves and not have to depend on anybody. Sometimes we have careers only because we have to and so the workplace becomes a place of struggle because it is not our ideal choice of a job. The other big mistake we make is that we categorize our careers as part of our 'secular' life, and we refer to our church activities as our 'sacred' lives. What is that all about? There shouldn't be a difference. Christian believers are to be the temple of God, so everywhere we go, we're supposed to take 'sacred' with us. Now if we are going to spend 8 hours of each day somewhere, God expects everybody there to experience the 'sacred' we carry! Our careers are not only a means of income! Our careers provide us with a means to be a blessing. Through the income we receive, we are able to bless our children, families, churches and communities. The knowledge we learn on the job gives us insight to be a blessing to others. We ourselves are to be a blessing to the people we meet on the job. The discipline we receive at work should train us to be disciplined in our relationships with others, in our interactions with other organizations, in our work at church. These are all aspects of the blessings our careers are to provide. If your career is not providing you with a means to be a blessing, or if you are not utilizing your job for such a purpose, then you need to rediscover why you are there. I love my career. But if it is not being a blessing to me, my family, my boss and my God then I need to reconsider this career. It is not just about a paycheck. It is about obedience to God. With or without a job, once I stay obedient to God at all times, I am assured that he will provide my needs. We must never be motivated just by the money. It should always be by what the Lord has mandated for our lives, first through the Bible, and also through the words that He speaks to us.

So think about this for a second, you working woman. What kind of career do you have and why? Is your career a blessing? If not, how can it be a blessing? Do you need to be in this career right now? Do you see the ministry in your career or not? Is it just a job, or is it a life-changing experience for you and the people you affect? If you are in any career for the wrong reason you will be imbalanced. If you are in the wrong career, you will be imbalanced no matter how much money you make.

4. Time - When I was a medical student, one of my professors made a passing statement to our class that changed my life. He said, "You need to decide now how much of your life you want to give to medicine." Why was that counsel so important? Because there are so many different paths in medicine, each with its own unique set of sacrifices and rewards. Neurosurgery is a long residency time, a huge time commitment, and a whole lot of money! Public Health is less clinical work, with more field and office activity. Then there is also where to work. Some hospital programs and jobs are much more demanding and time consuming than others. Some are prestigious and will beef up your resume for the rest of your life. Others have no pomp, but will give you just what you need to get you to where you want to go. Now my personal situation involved the ability to go for the prestige if I wanted it. After all, I could do it. I didn't have a problem with the hard work it would demand. I enjoyed the hustle and the bustle. But there was more than me to think about. I was called as a physician, but also as a wife (of a pastor, nonetheless!), and as a mother, and as church worker. I knew the prestige would cost me time with my family, and I had a four-week old baby. I knew it would take away from my ability to invest in our church. Another really important issue was that as much as I enjoyed my career and my ministry, my true sense of fulfillment at that time came from my baby! As I pondered this issue and looked at my life as a whole, and the things that were important to me at that point in time, I made choices that when put together allowed me to enjoy my life as a whole. So I gave up the prestige. I still had to work hard, but it was an environment of people who had other things to do besides being physicians. It freed me to stay very involved in my church, care for my son, and pursue my career as well. I learnt burnout and I learnt balance. I learnt hard work and I learnt rest. I learnt to give my best to others, and I learnt to ask others for help. And so now, it is a little easier to be a full-time doctor, mother, wife, church worker and writer all at the same time. It seems so impossible in the natural. But when you know what God has called you to do and you combine that with wise choices and timing, you will find that His will is never impossible.

In my situation, the balance of family was the constraining factor through which I made my choice. I used to erroneously say that if I had been single at the time, I would have gone for the prestige. That is another common and unnecessary mistake we make as women. We sometimes think that when we are single, we can do anything and move anywhere because we don't have the constraints of a family. But what if it is not the will of God for you? What if it is impractical? What if it is unwise? And even worse, what if it is unnecessary? A balanced woman is careful to use her time wisely. She is careful to spend her time doing the things that God has called her to do, not the things that just make sense to her.

So you have all the right reasons and have made all the good choices about life and career, and you have managed your time well. You need one last thing to succeed: a solid work ethic! How you work is just as important as what you do. Whether it's your career or your volunteer work, you have got to approach work with honesty, integrity and righteousness. These three things make up the seat of the well-balanced worker. Do you want to rock the worker hat? Wear it with balance!

Hats off to this worker!

OUR EXAMPLE – Rizpah

Do you know that one of the best signs of your work ethic is to examine how you work when you don't have to work? Yes, it is true. Rizpah didn't have to work. She was the king's concubine after all. She would be well taken care of for the rest of her life. But her world fell apart. There was a famine in the land because Israel had put Gibeonites to death despite their covenant to protect them. To make up for this, the Gibeonites wanted Saul's sons killed. So Rizpah's children (Armoni and Mephibosheth) were rounded up and killed, along with five of Saul's grandchildren. That was the end of it for everyone but not for Rizpah. She lay outside and protected the dead bodies from harvest time until it was sowing time again. She fought off birds and wild animals all day and all night, in the rain and in the sun just so they wouldn't touch the bodies of the royal young men. This act didn't matter to anyone else, but it mattered so much to Rizpah that she risked her life and worked day and night. Her reason, her choice and her work ethic lead her to spend all her time protecting dead bodies. Her actions were told to David. David was convicted, and decided to give King Saul, Jonathan and the slaughtered men the proper burial they deserved. Then and only then did the famine end. Thanks to the hardworking Rizpah!

Watch out for this worker!

OUR CAUTION - Martha

Martha was a well-known busybody and I must admit that I have a soft spot for her! I work hard to make sure everything is perfect, and my guests (and household) enjoy a good meal. Let's be real! I'm sure Jesus liked to have his chow when he came around, or Martha wouldn't have bothered with all the preparations! Interestingly enough, Jesus didn't tell Martha to stop cooking and come sit at his feet. Instead he emphasized that Mary's choice to listen to him should not be taken away from her. He said this, noting also that Martha was anxious about a lot of other things, when only one thing was needed. What is that one thing? To listen to Him. To hear Him. Is it possible to work and still hear God? As stated earlier, there is no such thing as secular and sacred for the Christian woman. If there was then we would have double personalities. We need to be excellent workers, and still be able to hear the voice of God while on the job. Martha knew how to hear Jesus, but she was distracted by the work. Do not let your job distract you from hearing what God has to say to you. Learn to live a life of listening to Him even while you're working.

This woman wore the worker hat in all the wrong ways!

OUR WARNING - Miriam

Miriam had a gift. She had a calling. She had a job to do, and she was good at it. When she picked up her tambourine to sing, dance and prophesy, the company of women would follow. She had a lot going for her, but there was one thing getting to her that she couldn't shake: she didn't like the boss's wife. And the boss was none other than her little brother Moses. So she began to murmur and complain against Moses' leadership. Miriam knew she was good, so why did she have the need to bring Moses down before she could appreciate the greatness of her gift? Ladies, if you are going to be an excellent worker, then never ever take your boss for granted! That was Miriam's first mistake. Here's another tip: People are slick! Don't think that if you go down, everybody else is going down with you. That was Miriam's second mistake. Maybe she thought her other brother Aaron would back her up and that would get her off the hook. Well, Aaron backed her up but it wasn't enough to save her. To make matters worse, Aaron himself didn't get punished! I'll have to ask God what really went down that day! For her role in this fiasco, God struck her with leprosy, she was confined outside the camp for a week, and the people could not move till her punishment was over. Miriam's imbalance, bad attitude and poor work ethic lead to a punishment that held the camp up. Our work as women should move people up, not hold them back. Our work should draw the pleasure of God, not the wrath of God. It is not uncommon to hear women say that they would rather work with men. That is a strong indictment against us, and the bad attitudes we can bring to work. It is time for Christian women to be true professionals on the job. You must reflect Christ in your ability to do your job and do it well. Don't let your good work breed ungodly pride in you, and you will reap the reward for your labor. Let Miriam be a reminder to you. You can be great all by yourself! Don't try to pull others down in an effort to prove your greatness!

This woman had the "O" factor!

She wore the worker hat with BALANCE.

OUR GOAL - Lydia

Thyatira was a wealthy town on the river Lycus in the Roman province of Asia. It was famous for establishing trade guilds that used natural resources of the area. The guilds were very organized, and closely associated with the Asiatic religions, making pagan feasts and immoral practices common. Lydia was a trader in purple dye, and probably a member of the guild there. She traveled a long distance to Philippi to trade, and probably lived in Philippi. In spite of the pagan religions she grew up around, she chose to worship God. She was at the riverside praying and made close contact with Paul, one of the greatest evangelists of all time. Lydia's faith was so obvious that Paul and his companions were persuaded to spend the night in her home. She secured salvation for her entire household, and in so doing exemplified the true purposes of our employment as Christian women: not only to provide financial gain to our households, but spiritual gain as well. The Bible says of her that she was a seller of purple who worshipped God. Her identity was not tied to one or the other. She wasn't a trader one day, and a worshipper another. She worked hard, and always worshipped. May we be known as the lawyers who worship God. The accountants who worship God. The secretaries who worship God. The housewives who worship God. The balanced workers who worship God. Amen!

CHAPTER THREE

THE DAUGHTER HAT

What has my experience as a daughter been like? Do I enjoy being a child? Who are my spiritual parents? What do I look for in a parent? Who have I adopted as parents?

Obaasima Principle: PRACTICE

The key to wearing the daughter hat well is to first be a daughter of God. When you know how to walk with God as your heavenly Father, you will be amazing as an earthly daughter!

1. You can't submit to your earthly parents until you have learned to submit to God

2. What are the rules that govern your relationship with God?

3. What are the rules that govern your relationship with your earthly parents?

4. Have you had enough practice? Have you passed the daughter test?

When Christians think of the rules of how daughters should relate to their parents, what probably comes to mind are scriptures about obedience and disobedience. Scriptures like these:

Ephesians 6:1-3 NIV

¹Children, obey your parents in the Lord, for this is right. ² "Honor your father and mother"--which is the first commandment with a promise-- ³ "that it may go well with you and that you may enjoy long life on the earth."

Proverbs 23:13-14 NIV

¹³Do not withhold discipline from a child; if you punish him with the rod, he will not die. ¹⁴ Punish him with the rod and save his soul from death.

Colossians 3:20 NIV

²⁰Children, obey your parents in everything, for this is pleasing to the Lord.

When a daughter is obedient, parents call her wonderful! It is great when a child is quick to obey, and extremely painful when it takes loads of energy to get a child to do what you want her to do. I think we would all agree that it is easy (as parents) to insist on obedience when we have the mind of God on a matter. When little Jill is reaching for a hot iron, we have no doubt in our mind that it is not in the will of God for her to get burnt. So we tell her to stop, and a wise daughter will listen and obey. Insisting on obedience is easy when the parent is right, isn't it? But parents aren't always right. What happens to the model of obedience in that case? Is a daughter always expected to obey even when the parent is wrong? Is it possible to be loyal to your parents even when you do not obey what they say? Other words for loyalty include: *faithfulness, devotion, allegiance, trustworthiness, constancy, reliability, fidelity, dependability, steadfastness.* Does loyalty go out the door when we fail to obey? And then there is the issue of discouragement and how we deal as daughters when we are discouraged. Even worse is how we deal when it is our parents who are causing our discouragement: Let's look at the scripture in Colossians again, but include the scripture that comes right after it:

Colossians 3:20-21AMPC

[20] *Children, obey your parents in everything, for this is pleasing to the Lord.*[21] *Fathers, do not provoke or irritate or fret your children [do not be hard on them or harass them], lest they become discouraged and sullen and morose and feel inferior and frustrated. [Do not break their spirit.]*

What becomes of the daughter who is being provoked or irritated by her parent? What becomes of the daughter who is fretting because of her parent? What becomes of the daughter who is discouraged, sullen, morose, feeling inferior or frustrated? What becomes of the daughter whose spirit is broken? Is it all about obedience for her too?

I wish everything was always as simple as telling a child not to touch a hot iron, but life presents issues that are much more complex than that. A daughter has to interact with more than just Mom and Dad. There are parents and step-parents. Biological parents and spiritual parents. Foster parents and adoptive parents. Mentors and coaches. Pastors and other leaders. Teenage daughters have another complicating factor to deal with called hormones and older daughters who are wounded have to deal with their broken hearts. Being a daughter is no easy task. As a daughter, how would you deal with the following situations?

- Parents disagree with your choice of friends and demand that you stop hanging out with certain people.

- Mom wants you to be a doctor, but you really want to be a nurse.

- Dad is away on business. You were never that close to Mom and you need someone to talk to.

- Pastor wants you to organize the church retreat, but you really need to go to Venezuela for the outreach program.

- Your parents do not like Greg. Greg is the man you want to marry.

- You feel so sad. All the parent figures in your life say it will just pass. But it hasn't.

- Coach wants you to take some vitamins. You have no proof that they aren't vitamins, but you don't feel right about it.

- Mom and Dad died in a car accident last year. You have lots of relatives, but you still feel alone.

- Mom is broke and wants you to send her some money but you are married now and have bills to pay.

- Your parents want you to discipline your younger siblings but you are just a kid yourself.

- Your parents/leaders are discouraged and need your help, but you are used to them helping you.

These situations are prime examples of why being a daughter is not just about obeying or disobeying. It is about making healthy choices in response to the information given to us by the parent figures around us while still taking responsibility for our actions. It is no small task. How do we handle these situations? How do we obey? How do we remain loyal while disobeying? How do we handle the discouragement we feel as daughters while still dealing with the pressures placed on us by the parents/leaders around us? How can we rock the daughter hat when it is so hard to keep our heads above water with everything else?

The best way to be an exceptional earthly daughter is to first be a daughter of God. When a daughter recognizes who she is in the heavenly courts of the King of Kings, her interactions with her earthly parents will take a beautiful turn. Throughout this book, we celebrate the roles women play. Each of the awesome characters recognized at the end of each chapter were first and foremost daughters of God. How they handled all their relationships on earth had a lot to do with how they handled their relationships with God. To wear the sister, worker, friend, wife, mistress, lover, rival, servant, mother, beloved, or rejected hat well you must first be a successful daughter of God. God is the parent who is always right. God's ways are always right. Loyalty to God guarantees us peace, joy, fulfillment and success in all that we do even when all hell is breaking lose. Obedience to God is the key to your success in any relationship.

There are many 'believers' in the world, but not many daughters. The church is full of women, but not many daughters. There are many who call themselves Christians, but there aren't many daughters of God. Daughters are easy to pick out. Anyone who knows my Dad can tell I'm his daughter just by looking at me. I look like my Dad. I walk like him. I inherited the gap in my front teeth from him. Look at my dimples, and you start to see my Mom in me too. The day we start to look like God, talk like God, act like God, interact like God, think like God, then we can call ourselves daughters of God. How do you gain such a resemblance to your heavenly Father? By surrounding yourself with Him. That means worshipping God. Reading the Word of God. Hanging out with other sons and daughters. It means talking to Him in prayer and listening to what He says. You want to look great in every hat you wear? Start today by being a daughter of God.

When you are a daughter of God, then the scenarios we looked at earlier in this chapter can be addressed from a different perspective. Let's look at how this played out in my own journey as a daughter with an earthly father and a heavenly Father. When I first became a Christian back in Ghana, I didn't know any other protocol about prayer except to put my feet up and talk to my Daddy God as if He was sitting in the ceiling looking down at me. I would even hold up my report card so He could see my grades! When I moved to the United States I went through a difficult cultural transition. In the midst of the difficulty, I stopped being a daughter of God even though I was still a Christian. What did that look like in real life? I surrounded myself with television and pizza instead of surrounding myself with God. I went to church on Sundays, but cried every other night of the week. I didn't talk to God the way I used to. I found my solace in food and gained a whopping 20lbs. When I started college, I met a wonderful group of young Christians and I rededicated my life to the Lord, and chose to be a daughter again. It was awesome! I started talking to Him again and even better I could hear Him speaking to me! I felt secure in God again but life wasn't perfect. I was still an 18yr old child living miles and miles away from home. I was lonely and every now and then I needed a home cooked meal from Mom but it was nowhere in sight. I couldn't touch my earthly parents, but I was a daughter of God, and I had peace from Him that I wouldn't trade for anything. I was doing really well in my classes. So well that the college gave me 24 AP credits so I could move into my sophomore year! It was unbelievable! Then came the bombshell: Dad wanted me to come back home to Ghana. Sounded like a great idea when I thought of how lonely I was, but as a daughter I was looking beyond my natural instincts to the thoughts and purposes of God for my life. When I prayed, I knew that God wanted me to stay. But my earthly father wanted me to go. What a conflict!

Somewhere we have it in our minds that once God tells us something, that means we can bully, connive, disrespect, or fight our way to get it. But an "O" Factor daughter of God doesn't operate like that. Disagreeing with (and yes, it does mean disobeying) your father, coach, step-mother, pastor or leader doesn't have to turn into a bloodbath, even if they become angry at you. Obeying God can cost us relationships, but let it not be said that our own bad character in the process is what really cost us the relationship, not the decision to obey God. So how was I going to disobey without disrespecting? Before I could come up with a solution for that, my father had already sent me a one way ticket to Ghana and I had one week to pack and leave! I called Daddy and tried to reason with him, but he had his mind made up. From his perspective, moving back to Ghana was the best thing for me financially and academically. I knew that if I chose to stay, I'd be on my own financially but I didn't have a dime. All I had was what my heavenly Father had told me and that was to stay in America. I calmly told Dad that paying for school wouldn't be a problem and that everything would be fine. He said ok, I hung up the phone, and then burst into tears! If Dad couldn't afford my education, I surely couldn't afford it either! But I knew what God had told me. The day for my flight came and since I hadn't packed, I figured there was no point going to the airport. I didn't have anything sensible to say to Dad, so there was no sense calling him back to let him know I had just wasted his money. So I delved back into heavenly daughter stance and went back to my Daddy God. I prayed and asked God for an answer. Much to my surprise, He actually started to give me some strategies to fund my education. I went back to the same people who worked with me and got me AP credit: my professors, my admissions counselors and my guidance counselor. They all attested that I was a student worth fighting for. Before I knew it, they hooked me up with 2 jobs, scholarships and grants that would pay for college! I ended up graduating from college completely debt-free! The other exciting thing for me at graduation was my admission to Johns Hopkins University School of Medicine. I would have never gotten into Johns Hopkins if I had moved back home. My father was so proud, and happy that I had stayed in the US. God proved his faithfulness. I could obey heavenly Father and disobey my earthly father without losing the relationship. I could disobey my earthly father without dishonoring or disrespecting him.

The essence of being a great daughter is to know how to tie your relationship with God to your relationship with your earthly parents. This takes wisdom and grace, both of which are available to us. Even

Jesus needed divine wisdom and grace to be an effective son.

Luke 2:49 NKJV

40 And the Child grew and became strong in spirit, filled with wisdom; and the grace of God was upon Him.

As a daughter, you must know the will of God for your life at all times. You must sharpen your ability to hear the voice of your heavenly Father. God wants to talk to you and love on you. He wants to heal every area of brokenness and pain in your life. He wants your spirit to be whole, so you can be of great benefit in the Kingdom of God. He wants to give you wisdom to deal with difficult situations. Maybe you've been a Christian for years, but you haven't known God as a Father. It's time to move into that new place with Him. Be a true daughter of God, then you can be a successful daughter of man. If you want to rock the daughter hat on earth, then you take the first step: practice by being a great daughter of God.

Hats off to these daughters!

OUR EXAMPLE - Miriam & Jephthah's daughter

Miriam gets an honorable mention as a daughter because she did something tremendous as a little girl. When little baby boys were being killed, Jochebed put her son Moses in a basket and laid him by the river banks. The Bible doesn't say what she told her daughter Miriam to do, but it does say that Miriam stood close by to find out would happen to Moses. Yeah, maybe we can assume Jochebed told Miriam to wait there. But who could have anticipated what would happen next? Pharoah's daughter came by and Miriam noticed that she had compassion on Moses. So Miriam, a little Hebrew girl, and daughter of Amram and Jochebed had the boldness to approach Pharoah's daughter. Pharoah's daughter had not even mentioned interest in doing anything with this child. It was Miriam who planted the idea in Pharoah's daughter that the baby could be hers. All she needed was someone to nurse the baby for her. And of course, Miriam offered to find a nurse to breastfeed the child for her. Wow! In so doing, she saved Moses' life AND created opportunity for Jochebed to be paid to be a Mom!! What a daughter!

Jephthah's daughter did no wrong. In fact, she did for her father what most Dads want: to receive a warm welcome whenever they come home. But as soon as she saw the look on her father's face, she knew that something was wrong. And when she found out that her father had promised to sacrifice whatever/whoever came out to meet him first, then she understood her father's distress. This girl recognized that obeying God was more important than satisfying earthly pleasure. This is the encounter in Judges 11:34 (NIV) when she realized that she would have to be sacrificed out of obedience to God. *"My father,"* she replied, *"you have given your word to the LORD. Do to*

45

me just as you promised, now that the LORD has avenged you of your enemies, the Ammonites." She took it a step further though. She chose to be a perfect sacrifice. Instead of asking for 2 months to get married or party, she asked for 2 months to remain a virgin. And when it was time, she willingly came back to be sacrificed. What an example! A daughter who allows her parents to obey God even if it will cause her pain! You can't do that unless you are satisfied and excellent as a daughter of God!

Watch out for this daughter!

OUR CAUTION – Herodias' daughter

Herodias' daughter lacked the wisdom to discern between good things from Mom, and bad things from Mom. It was her stepfather King Herod's birthday and this girl had danced her way into his heart. He was so pleased with her dance that he offered to reward her with anything she wanted, up to half of the kingdom. Half the kingdom? For real? My goodness this was a life changing opportunity! She could have become second to King Herod! There was so much at stake! So she did one very sensible that I will give her credit for: she sought counsel. She first left the room so she could talk to her mother Herodias. But that's just about all I will give her credit for because when Herodias told her daughter to ask for the head of John the Baptist, this girl just said, "Okay"! She rushed back to the banquet and asked that the head of John the Baptist be given to her 'right now'. She even added an urgency that her mother did not ask her to request. Did she not have the sense to know that it was wrong? Was life so meaningless to her that she could carry a human head on a platter and feel nothing? Was pleasing her mother more important than right or wrong? Would God not have honored this girl if she had refused to take this request to the King? The Bible does not applaud this girl as an exceptional daughter, and rightly so! This story would have had a different spin if Herodias' daughter was more eager to please her heavenly parent than her earthly parent. This story also illustrates why I'm confident that God doesn't expect us to blindly obey our parents even when they are asking us to do things that are against His will for us. She is a caution to us because she exemplifies the often difficult balance we walk when we seek to obey our earthly parents at the expense of obeying our heavenly Father.

This woman wore the daughter hat in all the wrong ways.

OUR WARNING - Athaliah

Athaliah was a terrible wife and mother because she started out as a foolish daughter. Athaliah was Jezebel's daughter. She grew up in the household of her parents Jezebel and Ahab, and must have witnessed her mother's angry tirades against Elijah, and her attempts to annihilate the prophets of God. The Bible records that Ahab was the most evil of kings. The actual description in the Amplified Bible

Classic Edition of 1 Kings 21:25 is that "there was no one who sold himself to do evil in the sight of the Lord as did Ahab, incited by his wife Jezebel." Ouch. She got an innocent man killed just so Ahab could have the field he wanted. This was the example of womanhood that Athaliah grew up around. When Jezebel heard that Jehu was coming and she was facing death, she painted her eyes and stood defiantly out of an upper window. She was pulled down and killed as she was run over by horses. Her flesh was eaten by dogs. Now, if I was her daughter, that alone would have been enough for me to say, "Er, I don't want that to happen to me so I'm not gonna live the way Mama did." Instead Athaliah chose to adhere to the wicked teachings and witchcraft of her mother. She became a power-hungry fiend of a woman because she never learned as a daughter how to glean right and reject wrong. Even though she was married to Jehoram, King of Judah, she managed to turn his heart towards Baal instead of towards God. When her husband and son died, she destroyed the royal family so she could rule herself. Think about it: she assassinated her own grandsons and took the throne for herself. She is referred to as a wicked woman in scripture, and her execution brought great rejoicing to the people. What a terrible reminder of what daughters should not embrace from their parents. What a crucial reminder that if we can perfect being daughters of God, we will be great at everything else, and if we flunk at being His daughters, we fail at everything else.

These women had the "O" Factor!

They wore the daughter hat with PRACTICE.

OUR GOAL – Esther, Rahab

Esther had every opportunity to be bitter: she was orphaned, and a slave in a foreign land. But she chose to remember that even though there was a lot she didn't have, she had God and she had a godly uncle Mordecai who had adopted her. He loved her, and she trusted him and the God he taught her to serve. In fact, she trusted him with her life, and he led her to the life of her dreams. He entered her into the beauty contest of a lifetime. The winner would become queen. Esther had practiced being a daughter of God and submitting to Him. She had practiced being a daughter to her uncle and submitting to him. So it was easy to obey the eunuch in the palace who told her what to do. Her obedience paid off. Can you say Queen Esther?!?!?! Oh yes, she won it all right, and all because she was an exemplary daughter who knew how to receive godly teaching from her heavenly Father, and all the parents He gave her on earth.

We don't usually think of Rahab as an exceptional daughter. In most sermons, she is the harlot who took the spies in and so her life was spared when the walls of Jericho came down. That is somewhat true, but I don't think she was spared because she took the spies in. I believe she was spared because she recognized that God was the great King over heaven and earth (Joshua 2:11, Hebrews 11:31). In other words, she chose to be a daughter of God in the midst of all of the chaos that must have been in her life. Because she was a daughter of God, she defied her earthly king and hid the spies. But when it came down to bargaining time, she didn't just bargain for herself. She bargained for the life of her mother, father, brothers and sisters. The deal was that she would have to house her family in her home and hang a scarlet cord out of her window. If any of her family members left out, they would be killed. Stop and think about this for a minute. The Israelites are coming and everyone in Jericho is afraid including Rahab's family. I wonder how she convinced all of them to come to her house and to stay there. Every day the Israelites were marching around the wall yelling and screaming and it must have been scary! Why stay? To the natural man it would make sense to try to run and hide and not just stay put in Rahab's house. She may have been a harlot with no regard by most people around her, but she clearly had some clout as a daughter of God and a daughter of man. She got her entire family to lodge in her home and they were safe. God was so impressed with this amazing daughter of His that He put her right in the lineage of Jesus Christ. What an honor! What a daughter!

CHAPTER FOUR

THE FRIEND HAT

Who are my friends? Who are my closest friends? In what ways have my friends hurt me? What special moments do I share with my friends? What do my friendships mean to me?

Obaasima Principle: SENSE

The key to wearing the friend hat well is to think before you act or react. Handle your friends just like you should handle your sisters: with sensible expectations!

1. Stop expecting your untrustworthy friends to be trustworthy.

2. Do not loan money to friends in need. They can't pay you back.

3. All friends are not created equal.

4. Friends are erring humans, just like you. Stop hating and forgive.

5. Develop a "no-nonsense" clause for your friendships.

Our natural mothers cannot be picked. Our sisters appear in our lives. Our co-workers move in to share our cubicles at work whether we like them or not. There are all kinds of women at church who we call our sisters, and we love them with the love of the Lord. But a friend is different. A friend is chosen. Friendship is one of the richest of all relationships, and a role that has incredible power. Friendship between women is especially profound because of our ability to connect with others, and our innate ability to talk and have deep relationships with one another. Just stop and think about that for a minute. Think about a couple of your female friends. Don't your thoughts bring a smile to your face? Even your memories of some of the fights you might have had make you laugh now! And yet, we often fail to enjoy the full blessing of our friendships.

LEVELS OF FRIENDSHIP

There is no one way to describe the friendship relationship because there are different levels of friendship. There are the acquaintances at our local grocery stores. We enjoy casual conversations with them as we pick out our fruit. There are the strangers we meet while we're getting our nails done. We hit it off immediately, and feel like we've known each other for years, yet, we never exchange phone numbers before leaving the nail parlor. There are also the co-workers we go out to lunch with every afternoon, who soon become good friends who only come by the house every now and then. And there are the other people we meet through all kinds of interesting circumstances, who truly become close friends and confidants. They could be sisters, co-workers, or indeed the lady we met at the nail salon. We talk constantly about everything and nothing, we hang out together, and truly enjoy each other's company. And even among such close friendships, there are still different levels! There are the close friends we pray with about deep issues, there are the close friends we can talk to about personal problems, and there are also the close friends we share ideas with without necessarily talking about our personal problems. But there are also people God brings our way as friends for divine purpose. We may not talk all the time or celebrate holidays together, but there is a divine friendship, and in specific seasons of our lives, those friendships meet the need for the season. And then there are also people whom God brings our way in order for us to pursue them for His divine purpose. In this case, we might be called to work hard at a friendship, (whether the other person works just as hard or not) because we are to meet a need in a season of their lives. Hmm. I know I hit a nerve there, and we'll talk about that a little later. We sometimes think that before we call someone a friend, there has to be this deep spiritual connection. Because of this erroneous notion, many Christians fail to nurture and develop their friendships with non-Christians around them. Now don't get me wrong. I'm not talking about relationships that can get us dragged into sin. I'm talking about being able to have a cup of coffee with your neighbor who is not a Christian, and still have a meaningful interaction that blesses both you and her, whether you talk about Christ or not.

How do you pick your friends? We sometimes base it on our similarities, and the fun things we can talk about or enjoy together. And so long as those common areas remain common, the friendship tends to go smoothly. But should she dare tick us off, we cross her off the friendship list, don't we? Should she mess up real bad, then the friendship is over. The marriage relationship also requires a choice, but to break it off, you've got to go through the courts. With friendship, we just write each other off as if the relationship never mattered. And yet, just like a marriage, broken friendships are often accompanied by broken hearts and wounded spirits. And then what happens after that? The wounded ones tend to wall themselves off and refuse to become close to another woman. And then bitterness can ever so easily set in. You know what happens after that? Even the Holy Spirit has a hard time permeating into the wounded one's world, because the wall is so thick and hard that even His voice cannot be heard. Only the voice of the pain and hurt, and it is that voice that dictates everything, not the Holy Spirit.

Each friendship is special and unique. We don't have to relate to all our friends the same way. The key for the "O" Factor woman pursuing godly relationship is to understand the purpose for each friendship God brings her way, and to use good old fashioned common sense to execute each purpose. When you understand the purpose of a relationship, then you can define appropriate expectations around the relationship. I have many friends who don't share my Christian beliefs but that doesn't change the fact that I love them and they are in my life to make me laugh! We talk about all kinds of things and have fun together but I would never go to those friends with a spiritual problem. I have friends who are members of my church who are in my life to help me have fun. I might go to the movies with them but I don't expect them to keep a secret about my marriage to their pastor. I have friends who are amazing Moms and we share parenting advice, but I don't loan them money because it is wrong for me to expect to be paid back! Hello? I'm their "mom-to-mom buddy" not their banker and besides, I don't have their credit reports so I don't know if they can pay me back! Here is the simple and blunt way to think about this: when you understand the purpose behind your friendships, then you can apply sense to the expectations you place on each friend.

SACRIFICE

True friendship takes sacrifice. To make a friendship work, somebody has got to be willing to do the hard work. And I am so sorry to burst somebody's bubble when I say this, but at any given point in time, one person is going to be making most of the sacrifices! I know, I know, we think it's supposed to be 50:50, but wake up and face reality. It is the same in marriage. Wouldn't it be great if both husband and wife made equal sacrifices to make the relationship work? But the reality is that at various points in all marriages, even when both are working hard at it, one person is putting in a little bit more, and tolerating a whole lot more to make things work. Friendship is no different. Can we all just get over this notion that if we are making all the sacrifices then the relationship isn't right? So many friendships have been broken because someone was no longer willing to make a sacrifice they were supposed to make.

Sacrifice takes many shapes and forms. Maybe you're always the first person to apologize. Or she never calls, you always do all the calling. Sacrifice could mean your time and money but the problem is usually not the sacrifices themselves. The problem is the same old issue of not understanding the balance between purpose, level of friendship, and levels of sacrifice. Some levels of friendship require a certain level of sacrifice and others just don't. Remember my example about my mommy-buddy friends? That level of friendship does not warrant the loss of my mortgage money! Just as there are levels in friendship, there are also levels of sacrifice. Be careful not to make the wrong level of sacrifices for a particular level of friendship. The worst part is that sometimes those high-end sacrifices end up enabling our friends to knowingly or unknowingly take advantage of us or become dependent on us in an unhealthy way. And it can sometimes get quite expensive! You know what I am talking about because you have lost some money to a friend or two. You see a friend in need, and you loan them some money, and the money never comes back when you need it, and you end up in a mess because of the sacrifice you made. In the end, the friendship suffers as well but it doesn't have to be that way. Know the purpose. Measure the level of friendship. Understand the commensurate level of sacrifice. Now use good sense and stay in your lane or you will regret it!

CONFLICT

The cold shoulder and silent treatment are hallmarks of female responses to conflict. I know that sometimes it truly is better to be silent, but I'm not talking about silence born out of wisdom. I'm talking about the silence that comes out of being hurt. It is accompanied by coldness and a sheer refusal to communicate and that is simply not of God. Can you imagine Jesus not talking to Peter over one of his (many) insensitive remarks? Okay, Jesus was a guy so maybe that's a bad example. How about if Mary Magdalene gave Pilate's wife the cold shoulder? That would have been weird, wouldn't it? So why should it be okay for other women of God like you and I?

Conflict is not pleasant at all. It is painful. Betrayal hurts real bad. When a stranger stabs us in the back it is annoying but not particularly painful. It gets on our nerves but it doesn't really hurt and we can move on in life. Betrayal hurts because it comes from a close one from whom you expect loyalty, and it is so hard to shake off. What do you do after you are betrayed, or hurt, or wrongly accused, or given the cold shoulder, or misrepresented, or treated unfairly, or overlooked, or whatever other painful experience your friend puts you through? What will your response be? How are you going to trust that God will not allow you to go through something you can't bear? Are you going to believe that God will cause this situation to work out for your good? Will you be able to rise above the feelings, and do what is right, or will you fall prey to the hurt and pain that cripple you and cut off the imminent blessing?

The principles of conflict management are clearly outlined in scripture, but when we are hurt somehow we don't want to believe that those scriptures apply to us! Look at what it says in Matthew 18 from the Message Bible.

Matthew 18:15-22 (MSG)

"If a fellow believer hurts you, go and tell him—work it out between the two of you. If he listens, you've made a friend. [16] If he won't listen, take one or two others along so that the presence of witnesses will keep things honest, and try again. [17] If he still won't listen, tell the church. If he won't listen to the church, you'll have to start over from scratch, confront him with the need for repentance, and offer again God's forgiving love. [18] "Take this most seriously: A yes on earth is yes in heaven; a no on earth is no in heaven. What you say to one another is eternal. I mean this. [19] When two of you get together on anything at all on earth and make a prayer of it, my Father in heaven goes into action. [20] And when two or three of you are together because of me,

you can be sure that I'll be there." [21] At that point Peter got up the nerve to ask, "Master, how many times do I forgive a brother or sister who hurts me? Seven?" [22] Jesus replied, "Seven! Hardly. Try seventy times seven.

This scripture is as plain as daylight: If a fellow believer hurts you, go and tell him (her) – work it out between the two of you. It even recognizes that it won't be that easy. Look at verse 16 - If he won't listen… Verse 17 – If he still won't listen….If he won't listen to the church. Okay, so I think the Lord understands that most of the people who hurt us won't listen to us, but He told us to go tell them anyway! And then verse 18 – Take this most seriously. As if the entire Bible is not serious enough, the Lord adds that we ought to take this most seriously. I think it means the Lord takes this seriously as well. It means every time we refuse to confront, He takes it seriously. He is watching. And then look at verse 20. And when we are not together, He takes it so seriously that He pulls away and won't hang around. Ouch! How are we going to live victorious lives if God has pulled out of our relationships? Before we try to say that this scripture doesn't apply to non-Christian friendships, don't forget that Biblical principles are principles of wisdom. They are principles that make sense! I can still use this as my response when my non-Christian friends offend me. Except for the part about taking it to the church of course!

The most exciting part about this conflict management protocol is in the very beginning: *If he listens, you've made a friend.* Wow! How true is that? I know I have had those experiences. When I approach someone about a problem and she listens, we get closer! There are two parts to her being able to listen (1) I have to say it in a way she can hear (2) She has to hear what I said. When you are approaching a friend about a problem, you have a big responsibility to communicate in a way that will be heard. I am very intentional about my communications, especially when I am upset. There are some emails that take me days to construct because I want to make sure it comes out the right way because I need it to be heard. When we aren't intentional about communicating to be heard, then our communications simply create more hurt and we end up losing a friend, instead of gaining one. Unfortunately there is another possibility: she does not listen. Sometimes we say it the best way we possibly could but she doesn't listen and we lose a friend. When that happens, be sure to continue to offer God's forgiving love.

TIPS FOR RESOLVING CONFLICTS

1. First of all, whether you are the 'hurtor' or the 'hurtee' you have got to listen and hear what the other person is saying, not what you are thinking. If someone is hurt, they're hurt! It doesn't even matter anymore what you meant or how you meant it. Someone is hurt and it's time to swallow your pride and repent for hurting your friend.

2. All you 'hurtees' out there will often discover that you are not the only one who has been hurt. You may have also caused hurt to your friend in that interaction. Be ready to swallow your hurt and pride as well and acknowledge where you went wrong. You may have gone to your friend to tell her she hurt you, but be ready to say you are sorry when you recognize where you went wrong as well.

3. When you listen, listen to the words that are said, not the emotions or antics that come with the words. Sometimes we get caught up in how she said it instead of being caught up in what exactly it was that she said. We've got to hear each other's hearts.

4. Talk to your friend alone first, not to other people. Choosing to talk to others instead of your friend is one of the biggest mistakes you can make when you are in the middle of a conflict. You only bring others into the problem if she won't listen. The other people you bring in are meant to be witnesses who can bring reconciliation, not people who just heard your side of the story who are there to back you up. Don't bring in 'witnesses' who are likely to agree with you and rub your backs and make you feel better about what you did wrong in the conflict, instead of challenging you to do the right thing. If you have to talk to somebody, then let it be someone you know will tell you the truth, and won't let you

get away with a lie. Talk to someone who will help you see the situation the real way, not in the "hurt fairy tale" way you have been looking at it. Talk to someone you will allow to help bring reconciliation. Talk to someone who will have the audacity to tell you when you are out of line. Talk to someone who will get you out of the enemy's camp if that's where you're lurking, and get you on the right track with the Lord and with your friendship.

5. I believe in self-examination and evaluation, but only for those who are not too critical of themselves. If you are extremely critical of yourself, you might get caught up in your mistake and put yourself down. Sometimes I can't trust my own assessment of myself in the midst of a conflict, so I get some mature, trusted friends to give me their opinion of my actions.

6. So if you've talked to your friend and she wouldn't listen, and you've brought in a witness to help and she still won't listen, that's when you bring in a higher authority like a parent or teacher or pastor etc. It is not the time to gather more witnesses and it is certainly not the time to try to prove to others that you are right and she is wrong!

7. It is a rare conflict where each person involved is saying the exact same thing. Most conflicts are also inflicted with lies,

exaggerations and misrepresentation. Be careful not to fall into sin no matter how hurt you are, because God expects the truth from us no matter how bad we feel. No matter how hurt you are, if you lie, God will deal with you.

8. In every one of us is the desire to be right and be the one who is apologized to, not the other way around. But we need to humble ourselves and be willing to do whatever it takes to bring peace, even if it means that we don't get the apology that is due us.

9. Avoid "You never" and "You always".

10. Don't bring up past issues unless they will help bring peace in this existing issue. If you didn't bring stuff up when it happened, then don't bring it up now!

11. Remember that even great friends can make great mistakes, and great mistakes require great forgiveness. Forgiveness is not for the 'hurtor'. When you, the 'hurtee' forgive, it frees you to enjoy life again and not be bound by the hurt.

12. Some hurts involve a broken trust, and it is difficult to bounce back as if nothing ever happened. Don't feel guilty about that. Give yourself time to heal and let the relationship grow again. Remember that forgiveness is different from reconciliation. Forgiveness is a decision that is independent

of the other person's feelings towards you. Reconciliation is a process that is very much dependent on both parties involved. During times of reconciliation, we often find that we have to go out of our way to do things to bring peace. So, for example, you might not feel like inviting her to your party but you do so anyway. And with time, the relationship will heal, and hopefully even be better than it was before. And even if the relationship never goes back to what it was before, you will be free from the wounds. If trust has been broken, allow trust to be reborn before making certain allowances. If she broke my trust by stealing my idea and presenting it as her own, then I might hang out with her, but my ideas stay with me!

13. What about if she won't listen to you and is spreading lies about you? It is only after you have obeyed all the Matthew 18 principles and done all of this (including forgiveness) that you can remind yourself that she is not the last friend left on earth! You can (and should) let her go. Don't waste time trying to prove that you are right and she is wrong, and please don't join her in spreading lies. Just move on.

TRIED AND TRUE

To develop a deep intimate friendship, the relationship must be tested and tried. The people I call my close friends today are people with whom I have had relationships for a very long time. We have been through things together, and we have been faithful to one another. We have hurt and have been able to forgive each other. We have made mistakes and have not been too proud to say sorry. We have cried together and laughed together. We have walked through each other's pain together. We have made sacrifices for each other - big sacrifices. We have been willing to sacrifice for each other even when we didn't have the means. We have kept each other secrets. We have respected each other's roles and responsibilities. We have stood beside each other even when we didn't understand each other. Yes, we have been mad at each other, and disagreed with one another, but we have learned to place high value on the relationship. Don't be in a hurry to be in a close relationship with someone when that relationship has not been tried, and has certainly not been found to be true. Remember the levels of friendship, and keep 'untried' friendships where they need to be. Trust is earned. Before you can trust someone as a close friend, they have to earn that trust, and we need to earn their trust as well.

I am a firm believer in giving a relationship time to develop and build. It is during this time that the purpose for the friendship will unfold. At the beginning the purpose might not be clear. You might just like her for no particular reason. So you call her, and send messages every now and then. Sometimes she responds, and sometimes she doesn't. When you know you like her for a divine purpose then it doesn't matter if she responds or not. You just keep getting in touch. Eventually, she connects with you and calls you. You start to spend time together and have fun together. It is during this time that you discover each other's likes and dislikes, mannerisms, preferences, idiosyncrasies etc. You learn how to respond and relate to one another in a manner that is fruitful. You recognize her weird ways and so you don't fuss when she is acting weird. In fact, you expect her weirdness and it doesn't bother you. With time, the person who started out simply as someone you liked becomes a close friend. But even those close friendships should have boundaries. All your close friends don't necessarily have to know everything about you, and your close friends don't necessarily have to save you to prove that they are close friends. Each friendship, the close ones and the simple acquaintances, have levels and boundaries that you must stick to in order to preserve them.

FORGIVENESS

Some relationships will be tried and found not to be true and that is a painful thing to go through. Sometimes we forgive our friends and give them chance after chance after chance and it leaves us frustrated. It seems like every day, one person is doing all the forgiving and when we get tired of forgiving, we just cut the person off. We lose many friendships because of this all or nothing approach. The woman of God who is seeking God's best for her friendships must understand that forgiveness is a basic part of the package but we need to develop skill in forgiving. We need to apply sense to how we forgive. Forgiveness means you free the person who has wronged you whether they are penitent or not. Forgiveness doesn't mean you have to go back to doing things the same old way. If you know your friend can't keep a secret, why make her your closest confidante and tell her things when you know she can't keep her mouth shut? Forgive her, but don't keep setting her up! Stop telling her juicy intimate details because she can't handle it! Yes she might come back and whine and cry because you didn't tell her all the details about your romantic night with your husband. It's like Delilah and Samson in Judges 16. She wailed, and wailed because he wouldn't tell her the secret behind his strength. But the truth is that she betrayed him time and time again. Samson forgave her for all the other times and she was still his wife, but Samson should not have trusted her with that information no matter what she said. She had been tried and found to be untrue time and time again. As you are forgiving, analyze the situation and determine how to move forward. Innocent mistakes that your friend is truly sorry for should not result in a totally revamped relationship, but other issues may require you to consider how you relate to that friend.

NO NONSENSE

We've talked a lot about applying sense to your friendships. I propose that our friendships also need some "no nonsense" or basic rules of engagement or they won't survive. These rules aren't commandments we get our friends to sign. No. They are our own rules for how we will conduct ourselves in a friendship. Those rules govern how we operate so that we do not compromise the friendship. Here are some of my rules.

1. I never loan money to friends. An unpaid loan can ruin a good friendship. I will only give money I can afford to lose if they can't pay me back.

2. My close friends are still human just like me. Appreciate more, expect less, and don't expect or need apologies.

3. There is no space in my heart or home for foolishness or foolish friends. Such folk can be acquaintances and we will still get along just find.

4. I will take the high road for friendships that matter, even when my friend messes up. I am a leader.

5. I don't need to cut my erring friends off. I just need to adjust the relationship.

Those are my rules and they have served me well. They were born out of painful experiences, and efforts to protect my little heart from being broken again and again and again. I realized that I was the one who was not applying sense to my friendships. I was the one who allowed anything and everything in and set myself (and my friends!) up for failure. I learned to apply sense to how I relate as a friend. Do I still get hurt? Yes. But the wounds are few and far between. Do you want to rock the friend hat? It takes sense. If it doesn't make sense, don't do it!

Hats off to these friends!

OUR EXAMPLE - Naomi's friends

Imagine the excitement when a good friend you haven't seen in ages is coming over. You can't even sleep the night before she arrives. You tell everybody about this friend and all the good times you had together. You so look forward to being together that you can't sleep! You are up all night reminiscing about the 'good old days' and can't wait to catch up on each other's lives. And then when she arrives, you almost can't believe it's her! Especially if she looks and acts the way Naomi did when she came back from Moab! She looked different, and she sounded different. She came back a bitter woman, and she said so herself. "Don't call me Naomi!" she said to her old friends, "Call me Mara!" Interestingly Naomi means *pleasant*, while Mara means *bitter*. Hmm. What do you do with that bitter friend or the one who always has an attitude or that other one who just isn't acting right? How about the lady who always has issues, and is extremely difficult to deal with? And then there is also the friend who is going through some stuff and demands a whole lot of patience, love and attention, and is probably not going to give back a lot of patience, love and attention to you? Many of us would fall under the pressure and just steer clear of that friend because she can drain the life out of anybody, but not Naomi's friends. They stood by her through her bitter phase and were still there with her when she got her breakthrough. We all want friends like that, but which of us is willing to be a friend like that for somebody else? Naomi's friends are an example to us, because they persevered in friendship even when it might have seemed like they were giving a whole lot more than they were getting.

Watch out for these friends.

OUR CAUTION - The Daughters of Jerusalem in Song of Solomon

> **Song of Solomon 5:9** *What is your beloved more than another beloved O fairest among women? What is your beloved more than another beloved that you charge us so?*

> **Song of Solomon 6:1** *Where has your beloved gone, O fairest among women? Where has your beloved turned aside, that we may seek him with you.*

Let's paraphrase the first scripture: "What's so good about your man, oh beautiful one? Why is he better than anyone else, and why are you trying to counsel us? You can't even find your man!" And then after she tells them all about her man comes the second scripture. Let's paraphrase that one too: "Oooooooo, he sounds cute, girlfriend! I'll help you find that man! Where is he?" Did you notice how fickle these friends are? One minute, they didn't have time for her stories, and the next minute they're so interested in hearing about him? Let's see, how can I say this? Watch out for friends who want your man!!! Enough said!

But there are other aspects of this friendship to watch out for. What if the beloved didn't have a good explanation for these friends? Would they have still gone with her to help her find this wonderful man? Can we be good friends even when it demands our time and energy? And think about it, the explanation she did have, was just a description of his physical characteristics and that was good enough for them! We need friends (and we need to be friends) who will not be satisfied with just the physical, but who will push for excellence in the things of the Spirit. And one more thing about these friends. I think those daughters of Jerusalem must have been a little hard-headed! Why? Because in the 8 short chapters of the Song of Solomon, this verse *"I charge you daughters of Jerusalem, do not stir or awaken love until it pleases"* appears 4 times! (2:7, 3:5, 5:8, 8:4) It sounds like these girls were chasing after love in all the wrong places at all the wrong times! And the beloved had to tell them over and over and over and over again not to do that. Friends like that will wear you out! It can be exhausting, but don't give up on them, and don't be like them! Keep your relationship with the Lord fresh so you have a word to speak into their lives as often as necessary! This relationship is a caution to us because it was right on that thin line, and had great potential to tip over but fortunately, it did not!

These women wore the friend hat in all the wrong ways.

OUR WARNING - The housemates

If you haven't done so already, please read the story in I Kings 3. These friends (Let's call them Jill and Jane) were housemates, and both were pregnant at the same time. They delivered their babies within days of each other. One night, Jill her accidentally rolled over her baby and the baby died. So she got up and switched the babies, but lied and insisted the living baby was hers. They took their case before King Solomon, and each insisted the living baby belonged to her. So the king decided that the living baby should be split in two. Jane was willing to let her child live, even if she couldn't have the child. Jill preferred that the child be split in two. That way, neither of them would have him. Can you tell who the real mother was?

There is a time for friends to enjoy shopping together and owning similar things, having their kids grow up together, etc. But a friendship that only thrives on those common areas is a farce because sooner or later, those common areas will change. What if your best friend never gets married but you do? What happens when your friend chooses to do certain things with other friends instead of you? What if you never have children but your best friend does? In this story, Jill would only be satisfied if neither she nor Jane had the pleasure of the child. She couldn't handle seeing her friend enjoy something she couldn't have. So she stole her friend's baby. She stole him. She maliciously took something that was precious to someone who was supposed to be her friend. True friendship gives, and makes sacrifices. It does not take, grab or demand. Jill was clearly not a true friend. Jane on the other hand was willing to sacrifice so her child could live. See, this is the issue - she was <u>willing</u>. When we make sacrifices for our friends it has to come from a willing heart. Don't give up things for your friends grudgingly and then get upset because things don't work out the way you thought they would. Jane was willing to give up her baby because it was the only option to save her child's life. Before you go out there and sacrifice something that precious, understand that the alternative was that the child would die. This level of sacrifice was necessary for the life of her child. You must help your friends, but don't make unnecessary sacrifices in a friendship. Jane was a true friend and a true mother. Because of her willingness to sacrifice for the sake of the child, the king recognized that she was the true mother. Like the king, God is watching us. He is evaluating our emotions, thoughts, attitudes and motives. The Bible doesn't say what happened to this friendship

73

after the king's verdict. I'm sure Jane moved out! But Jill's actions in this so-called friendship are a warning to us because friendship gives. It does not steal.

OUR WARNING - Euodia & Synteche

Another warning to us is the story of Euodia and Synteche, two ladies memorialized in scripture as the feuding Christian leaders. Paul had so many important things to write to the Philippians, yet he had to use one line to urge these Christian women to stop arguing. How embarrassing is that? So to all you feuding friends out there. Here's a word to the wise straight up from Paul: Be of the same mind in the Lord!

These women had the "O" Factor!

They wore the friend hat with SENSE.

OUR GOAL - Jesus' posse

Mark 16:1 (NKJV)

Now when the Sabbath was past, Mary Magdalene, Mary the mother of James and Salome bought spices, that they might come and anoint Him.

Luke 8:1 (NKJV)

Now it came to pass, afterward that He went through every city and village, preaching and bringing the glad tidings of the kingdom of God. And the twelve were with Him, and certain women who had been healed of evil spirits and infirmities – Mary called Magdalene, out of whom had come seven demons and Joanna the wife of Chuza, Herod's steward, and Susanna and many others who provided for Him from their substance.

When friends come together to promote the gospel, incredible things always happen. Mary Magdalene was a former demon-possessed woman. Joanna's husband Chuza was not a steward in the sense of a servant. He was the manager of the Herod's household. Little is known of Susanna. Mary (the mother of James) is probably the wife of Clopas, and is believed to be the mother of Jesus' brother James. Salome is believed to be the mother of James and John, and the wife of Zebedee. Look at their backgrounds! The gospels describe all kinds of squabbles in which the disciples found themselves. But nothing of the sort is described in terms of these women's relationship with each other. How in the world were these women able to join together in spite of their differences? I really believe that they applied some of the principles we have discussed in this chapter. They created appropriate boundaries and had a straightforward approach to how they would manage their issues. They were funding the ministry of Jesus! There was a cause much bigger than their issues. So they came together as one and propelled the purpose of

God forward. That is the ultimate purpose of friendships involving Christian women: that we would relate to our friends in a manner that advances God's purpose in their lives and ours.

CHAPTER FIVE

THE WIFE HAT

Are you a happy wife? Do you hope to get married one day?

Is marriage okay? Are you struggling after being divorced or widowed? Are you just tolerating marriage? What kind of wife do you want to be?

Obaasima Principle: ENDURANCE

The key to wearing the wife hat well is to be able to handle pressure. Being a wife is no easy task. You have to be prepared to do the work it takes to find the right husband, wait for the right time, and handle all the drama that the wife hat comes with! A wife needs endurance!

6. Pick this hat with great wisdom. It's for strong women only.

7. If you picked it, you picked it. Make it work as best you can.

8. Pick your battles. People with happy marriages don't sweat the small stuff.

9. Say "no" to abuse.

1. If the hat comes off, you're going to need endurance more than ever before

The wife hat is unique; very different from any other hat you will wear. First you get a license. Well, hopefully before you get the license you meet a guy and fall in love! Then you go into a defined setting like a church or a courtroom or a beach if you are so inclined! There are officials and witnesses in that setting, where you verbalize your intention to become a wife for richer or for poorer, in sickness and in health or whatever vow you make. The documents are signed, the official makes a statement and the wife hat is placed upon your head by law. The hat almost always looks good when you put it on initially and there are lots of great hat days. For those who work extra hard at their hats, things are fairly okay. But even for the best of wives, sometimes this hat gets really heavy. It weighs on your head and you want to take it off for just a few minutes but here is the kicker: you can't take it off! The hat stays on even when you are upset. Sometimes the hat gets dirty and very unattractive but you still can't take it off. Sometimes the person you vowed to be with forever is the very person beating at your hat, but you still don't have the power to take it off yourself. You can fire your friends and you can quit your job, but you can't take the wife hat off. To take this hat off, you have to go to court, cite reasons, file documents, and wait for a period of time. That sounds like a whole lot of drama but guess what? There is much more.

Being a wife is hard work. The wife hat is so hard to keep pretty because it's not just up to you. There is a partner in the picture who either helps or hurts the cause. An emotionally strong and hardworking husband depends on his wife's strength. He needs her love and constant admiration. He feeds off of her strength so he can stay strong and keep going. An emotionally weak and lazy husband depends on his wife's strength too. He needs her strength to hold the family together so he can stay alive and keep doing nothing. And because women are problem solvers by nature, we come into marriage with a strong work ethic regardless of which man we marry. We handle the marriage, family and life the best ways we know how, but it gets exhausting even for women who thrive on being needed by the people around them. Many women strive to be emotionally, physically and spiritually strong all the time. In our moments of weakness, we look around us for help but today's society projects a false image of what a wife is. The good examples seem to be few and far between. The wife on the soap opera is gorgeous! She has 3 children but still has the body of a 17 year old. Every wife watching her wants to look like that! But in addition to her amazing body, she is devious and conniving; because that's the only way she can get what she wants. It's hard to admire her beauty and want that part of her without also admiring her naughtiness. News stories and bits and pieces of information gathered from today's social media environment give us continuous insight into horrible marriages. It looks like everyone in Hollywood is getting divorced, so we look to the holy places for hope, but it seems like all the Christian marriages are struggling as well. To make matters worse, our friends, relatives and neighbors are also having challenges in their marriages, so it seems to underscore the falsehood that marriage is painful, being a wife is horrible, and anyone who says they are happy is lying. With that perspective, the moments of weakness can expand into a lifetime of struggling to find relevance and meaning in your role as a wife.

Unless we discipline ourselves in this 'free' society and protect ourselves from false images, we will never believe in the biblical version of marriage. We will evaluate God's principles through the eyes of the world, instead of by the Holy Spirit. We cannot come to understand or practice the role of a Christian wife if we are going to the Lord with a soap opera image of a wife. The biblical view of a godly wife will seem strange to you if all you know is the pain your mother suffered as a wife. If the drive for 'girl power' is what consumes you, then you will always chuckle and shake your head in derision at the thought of submitting. If your marriage is failing right now and you believe you've already tried God's way, then the Bible will become a closed book; you will not find the help you are looking for, because your perspective is that God's way isn't working. When I'm going through a rough time, it affects how I function. My tendency is to tough it out at work and everywhere else except at home. At home all the emotions come out and I take 'life' out on the person I vowed to love and live life with. Am I the only person who does this? Somehow I don't think I am. The wife hat gets heavy even for folks with great marriages, because life itself weighs on the hat. When the kids get sick, or debts pile up, or things get complicated at work, that's when the wife hat gets heavier and heavier. It is hard to be a 'happy wife' going about your business when life isn't what you want it to be. The craziness of life seeps into our marriages, and instead of husband and wife building together and climbing out of trouble, we take out our frustrations on each other, and sink deeper into trouble. What should we do instead? How can we wear this wife hat successfully? How do we get back on track? How do we forge ahead towards a good-looking wife hat? How do we embrace and practice the "O" Factor principle of endurance? That depends on where each wife is in her quest for success.

The Okay Wife

So you haven't considered divorcing or killing your husband, at least not lately! You love your man and while life could be a little bit more exciting, it really isn't horrible. You have the routine down and everything is okay. How does an okay wife shift the gear into a new level? Here is what you do: you apply your strength towards maintaining your friendship and love relationship with your husband. You can't use up all your energy on the kids, the budget and the timeline you mapped out when you got engaged. Invest some more energy in your relationship with him. Get back to being friends and doing what friends do: they take a break from life to hang out and have fun together. There is no honey-do list, no demands from the boss and no screaming children. The okay wife needs to take a chill pill every now and then, hang out with her husband, and create some moments of joy and laughter in the midst of the routine of life. You can't be a helpmeet to your husband if you don't have a relationship with him. You can't add to his life if you don't like him. After years of marriage, the things you used to tolerate in him can become annoying and you will lose your 'like' for him. Little by little, this 'lack of like' leaches into the relationship and it becomes unfulfilling and boring. The wife hat gets quite crooked when we wear it without a true relationship. Ephesians 5:33 gives the okay wife some interesting marching orders about how she should treat her husband in this relationship. It is beautifully spelled out in the Amplified Version: *"..and let the wife see that she respects and reverences her husband [that she notices him, regards him, honors him, prefers him, venerates and esteems him, and that she defers to him, praises him, and loves and admires him exceedingly.]"* Wow. God requires of you that you notice your husband's haircut. Stop whatever you are doing with the kids and admire your man. If you prefer him above other men then choose to gaze at him instead of those TV marriages that even you cannot live up to. You must lay those images aside and defer to him, recognizing that he's all the man you're ever going to get. Even if you think you married the wrong man, you're married to him now and he is your husband. Choose to acknowledge and admire the good that your man does, and do it exceedingly, instead of being focused on the mistakes he makes. Esteem him even when he doesn't deserve it. Respect him as your husband and love him exceedingly. Don't you think it's a whole lot easier to desire, give, and enjoy sex with a man you love exceedingly? Isn't it easier for you to submit to a man when you actually admire him? You are able to share with him and entrust him with your life because you prefer him. Is this scripture for real? *..and let the wife see that she respects and reverences her husband [that she notices him, regards him, honors him, prefers him, venerates and esteems him, and that she defers to him, praises him, and loves and admires him exceedingly.]*" That is powerful stuff! It takes a strong woman to be able to love a man like that. You need the ability to endure when the man you are preferring and venerating might not even notice it. He might snore so hard at night that admiring him at two o'clock in the morning is going to be pretty difficult! Only an enduring wife can see past the annoyances and still admire him. When you make it a point to reverence him then this is getting serious! Some wives can't even comprehend what it means to revere a man and treat him as holy. You can't relate to your husband in the Ephesians 5:33 way unless you have a real Ephesians 5:33 love relationship with the Lord. There are a lot of women prancing around church, but few who love God like that. Until you learn to be in a love relationship with your God, you will never know how to truly love a man the way God intended. Let me spice it up a bit: until you know how to really worship the Lord and be caught up in His love during worship, then your bedroom worship with your husband will never be rich and full the way God intended. Until you know how to cry out to God when you're hurting, you will continue to play those silent treatment tricks with your husband, and that is NOT the way God intended marriage to

be. Until you know how to obey the Word of God when it hurts, it
will always be hard to submit to a husband whose demands are not
easy. Hmm. Until you know Jesus as the lover of your soul, you can't
even accept yourself enough to give yourself to your husband the
way God intended. Furthermore, if you don't understand the value
God places on you, you give yourself away freely to any man who
wants a piece of you. You diminish your value, and give yourself to a
husband who was not meant for you, a man who can't handle you or
a guy who won't propel you. Do you want to shift things up a gear as
an okay wife? Then get back in love with God and watch Him turn
your love for your husband into gold.

The Happy Wife

Some of you don't want to read this because happy wives get on
your nerves. As with everything else in The "O" Factor, let me
challenge you a little bit. The happy wife isn't the woman who is
happy because she has it all. She is happy because she endures and
keeps it all. She doesn't give up when times get hard. She doesn't
shrink back when plans don't work out. She doesn't give up on God
because she still can't conceive. She chooses to still consider her
hubby sexy despite his new potbelly. Many couples laugh at
newlyweds because they are so in love and it becomes almost
annoying to old married couples. But ask yourself this, why did your
honeymoon end? I'll tell you why: it ended because you let it! You
came home from Jamaica, went back to work and let life eat at you.

The happy wife endures. She brings Jamaica back home with her, and works hard to keep Jamaica around even when the marriage seems to be in Jericho! Some Christian women talk more to their Bible study friends than they do to their unsaved husbands because 'he won't pray with me.' Hello? He is still your husband, your best friend, and your confidante! You can be happily married even if your beliefs and convictions vary. The happy wife brings that anointing home from church and ministers it to her husband not just by praying for him, quoting scripture, and telling him he ought to go to church, but by loving him and honoring him as her husband. Can you imagine a woman who comes home from a revival meeting, goes to her unsaved husband, tells him how much she loves him and then makes love to him? He's going to wonder what happened at that meeting! He might even send her back again, or better still, he might go with her! The happy wife makes time for her marriage no matter what else is happening in life. She keeps Jamaica around, even when all those little people come around and crowd up the honeymoon suite. She nurtures the relationship through the changes and keeps the focus on God. She communicates effectively, and does not give way to the devil. She does not give way to offense, but rather gives way to the Spirit of God! What does that mean? It means that she doesn't sweat the small stuff or hold on to unnecessary offences. She makes herself the vehicle for positive change instead of being the one who points out all the negative. She may not have it all together, in fact many parts of her life and marriage may be awful. But she makes the most of it all the time. That is one happy wife.

The Wife-Want-To-Be

It is better to be single than to be in a miserable marriage. I know it is hard for a single woman to hear that from a married woman but it is true. All over the world are wonderful Christian women who made the fatal decision to marry a man who was not the right choice for them. They do it because they've finally found someone who makes them feel good and they are tired of feeling bad or they just don't want to be alone anymore. The whole relationship is not linked to prayer, the will of God, or godly wisdom, but to a feeling. And then weeks, months or years down the line, the feeling isn't there any longer. The thrill is gone and misery seems to be eternally present. I personally believe that for every two women who get divorced each year, there is another married woman who is considering divorce, and another one who thinks about it at least once a the year! While you still have the blessed opportunity of choosing whose wife you will be, ensure that you make that choice with biblical wisdom and careful consideration. If he does not satisfy biblical criteria and you go say "I do" to him, then you are asking for it. In God's marriage math $1 + 1 = 1$. If you are not a whole person and you marry a guy who is half a Christian man, see what happens: $1/2 + 1/2 = 1/4$! You both get drawn down and you, oh wife, do not fulfill the purpose for which you were brought on the scene. And you ladies who want to marry your dream man. You know, the one who is going to make you a better person. $1 + 1/2 = 1/4$. You are going to drag him down, and you're going to move a little further down in the process too!

When Hosea married a prostitute it was to fulfill a prophetic mandate. It was not because he hoped she would change one day. DO NOT use Hosea as your reason to marry someone who doesn't match up to you emotionally and spiritually. Check the man out before you decide you're in love with him and want to marry him. Is he rude to his colleagues? Does he ignore people who need help? Does he ignore rules and boundaries? If he does these things but you don't, then why in the world do you think he will match up to you emotionally? Sometimes we become so spiritually-minded that we lose our sense of practical wisdom. A dear friend of mine broke off a relationship because she determined the man wasn't really a Christian. When I asked her how she figured it out, she gave me the simplest and yet most profound answer I have ever heard. She told me the Bible he supposedly had for years didn't have a scratch in it. It was clear to her that he got it just to impress her and make her think he was a strong Christian man. Wow. You need to watch the man you want to marry. And don't just watch him by yourself. Be like Rebecca who allowed her family to check Isaac out and determine that he truly was the right man for her. Allow your family, friends, pastor and other trusted leaders to check him out. These are the people who know you and will tell you the truth. Listen to their counsel. If they have concerns then you better listen carefully and be sure about what you are getting into. You cannot be an exceptional wife if you don't have an exceptional husband to receive you. Don't marry a project – a fixer-upper.

Single ladies, you have a wonderful advantage because you still have the chance to get yourself right, and then choose the right guy to marry! There are many married women who didn't know better when they were single, and made choices they now regret. Pledge to yourself that you will not schedule yourself for unhappiness by choosing the wrong man or the wrong time. Use your time of being single to pursue God like never before. Fall in love with Him, and obey His commandments. Then you will find he who was handpicked by God just for you!

The Widowed Wife

Rarely is a wife ready for her beloved husband to die. No one is ever prepared for what this means. What does she check off the next time she fills a form that asks for her marital status? What does she do when her married friends invite her over but she feels like she no longer fits in? Without her consent, her wife hat has been yanked off her head. Is she still a wife? No, you say? Then can someone explain the intense love she still has for her husband? Can someone explain the emotional and physical longings that continue even after he is gone? How does a woman remain strong when the love of her life is no longer physically present on earth? How does she trust God again? How does she regain her lost strength?

The widowed wife must mourn. She must acknowledge her grief and actually walk through its stages: denial, anger, bargaining, depression and acceptance. Because women are all different, there is no uniform timetable to move from denial to acceptance. This means that a widow's friends and relatives must be patient in the process and understand the dynamics of her life. The acceptance phase doesn't mean she is now okay with it. No. It just means the widow is ready to face what has happened and start living again. It can be riddled with the pain of reality: having to pack things, move, make career changes and whatever else a widow ends up having to do with her new reality. That new reality could include waves of tears, a deep pain in the chest, a faith that is bruised and bystanders who don't quite get it. It is a prolonged traumatic experience that is not easy to survive. It takes even more endurance than ever before. In Ghanaian culture, death and mourning is taken quite seriously. There is a set number of days of mourning and a set time a widow must wear black and remain in mourning. Eventually, the time of mourning is over and she must take off her black clothing. This model of grieving is interesting and insightful. It reminds me that a widow must grieve, but must also ultimately embrace the massive shift that has taken place in her life and choose to live. She must ultimately learn to believe in herself and her God again. She will do this by remaining strong in her faith, and surrounding herself with people who will propel her to stand. She will not be ashamed to get professional help like counseling and other support. She will take a day at a time, a breath at a time. And if she so desires, she will love again. Yes, she will!

The Unhappy Wife

After an initially blissful time, marriage is now rough. You may have made all the right choices in a spouse, but somehow things have changed. Something happened. It might have even been something good that became a snare in the marriage. He has changed, or you have. Maybe you both ignored the warning signs. Or you became a Christian after you got married to a man who seemed perfect for you then. Maybe you made the fatal mistake of marrying someone you knew was not God's choice for you. And now, you find yourself in a marriage that is not the marriage of your dreams. There are many different scenarios that can result in unhappiness. Maybe you are truly miserable, broken and hurt, but have nowhere to go and nothing left to try. Or you might not be thrilled with your marriage, but you can handle it. There are just one or two things that aren't the best, but you can live with it. Others are actually unhappy, but can still choose to stay put. And another group in this category have their bags packed and one foot out the door. Any woman, Christian or not, who is caught in a difficult marriage deals with deep pain and desperation. Unfortunately, there is no easy way out of this pain. For the Christian woman in this situation, there is only one way out.

My son has a special hug he gives to people in whom he delights. He calls it a squeeze hug. In order to receive my son's special squeeze hug, you have to be in position. Your arms have to be open and your legs have to be astride or you will get knocked over. And you have to be ready to smile. It is the same with the Lord. He has a squeeze hug for you, but you have to be in position to receive it. You have to be in a posture of receiving from Him. The psalmist said in Psalm 94:19 *"When anxiety was great within me, your consolation brought joy to my soul."* When you are in position, then His comfort will delight your soul in spite of the great anxieties you are facing. It is only in seeking Him that you can be healed of the hurt you have suffered during the pain of your marriage. And let's get this straight: you need to be healed. The disappointments, pain, abuse and strife that occur in a broken marriage also eat away at us spiritually, and we need a healing, a cleansing in our body, mind and spirit. Many times when we get to the rough roads of life and marriage, we become spiritually dry because we feel like we are all prayed out. In I Samuel 1 Hannah refused to be all prayed out. She was broken hearted, but she kept going, she kept praying, she kept crying, year after year. She kept suffering year after year. And she kept right on praying. When you have put yourself in a posture of waiting on God, then you are ready to receive from Him. That's when you prove to Him that you trust Him. You can't trust someone you don't know. Your trust in the Lord is what will keep you going, when nothing else in your marriage seems to be moving. Even when everything in your marriage is going

91

great, your trust in Him will remind you that all is well because of God, not because of the awesome man you married! When you trust God, then you can obey his Word about marriage, even when it hurts. When you are truly in love with the Lord and have learned to talk to Him, and listen to Him, sooner or later, He's going to tell you a few things about your husband! When you are just fuming with anger and the Lord whispers a gentle word of calm into your spirit, and sometimes even tells you your husband is right, it's a little easier to let go of the offense. When God shows you His view of your husband, it is easier to hang in there just a little longer. But this kind of information doesn't just come because you went to church this week. It comes to people who are ready for a 'squeeze hug'. It's easier to love people when you see them through God's eyes. When you learn to truly trust God, you are able to trust the biblical wisdom and knowledge you need to be the kind of wife He wants you to be to a man who may not be all that he could be.

So go back to that love affair with God. Before you start praying for your spouse to change or making decisions about how to fix your marriage, YOU need to get back into God. Refocus on Him. Cry out to Him. Worship Him. Rediscover His love. Get back into eating the Living Word. Go back to church. Find strong women who will challenge you in your faith and rebuild your relationship with Jesus. Get out of living in pain, and resume living in God. Despise the shame of your pain, and choose to serve God. When you have been able to turn your focus away from the hurt and to God, then you can safely assess your situation and come up with the right solution. What exactly is it that needs to change in your marriage? Be real. Be specific. Be brutal. Start first with yourself. Dwell on the things you have control over, not on the past mistakes that cannot be changed. Even if your husband never changes, what can <u>you</u> do to restore your joy in the marriage? Rediscover ways to speak to your husband so this time, he actually hears and listens. Go back to honoring your husband in spite of himself. Go back to entrusting your marriage to the Lord through the good times, and the bad times.

The Divorced Wife

Very few marry with divorce in mind but sometimes it happens. Sometimes it has to happen to fully break ties with someone you must be separated from physically, emotionally, legally and functionally. I don't know anyone who has enjoyed divorce. Do you? For most people, both men and women, it is an extremely painful ordeal. The last thing a divorcee needs is to be questioned by folks who have no clue. So I'm not going to interrogate you, I'm just going to encourage you. God has love and compassion for his daughters who have had to go through the painful experience of divorce. Many people may not understand you. You might have even lost many Christian friends because of your divorce. Life has taken on a whole new meaning but listen to this: God did not divorce you when you got divorced from your husband. You lost your footing but all hope is not lost. This is how you survive and rise above. First you surround yourself with hope. This is not the time to be around people and situations that bring you down. Rather be with people who promote the best in you. This is key. Don't just choose people who make you feel good. Choose people who propel you to be your best. Secondly, get your physical strength back. Exercise, take walks and eat well. You have a new life to build and it will require physical strength. And finally, get your emotional strength back. Build on the hope you surround yourself with and start to hope again yourself. Learn to trust yourself, but more importantly choose to trust God again. God still has a plan and hope for your life if you will allow Him to give you the squeeze hug and breathe life back into you. You are in a new chapter of life. You may not have asked for it, but you get to write it and not make the same mistakes as before. Make it a good chapter!

The Abused Wife

Abuse occurs in marriage when one spouse uses their strengths, control and power to diminish the value of the other spouse. It is not a consequence of wrong behavior on the part of the abused. It does not just go away because the abuser said, "I'm sorry." It is not a problem just for poor, struggling, minority couples. There are male abusers and there are female abusers. Abuse has found its way into many Christian marriages, even amongst Christian couples in church leadership. It has no respect for race, culture, age or class.

Unfortunately, it is not uncommon. Abuse comes in many forms:

- Emotional Abuse - threats, insults, jealousy, ridiculing, lying, broken promises.

- Physical Abuse - shoving, restraining, kicking, weapon-use, physical harm, failure to physically assist the other.

- Sexual Abuse - rape, non-consensual sex/sexual acts, criticizing, using sex as a weapon, manipulating for sex, purposefully inflicting STDs.

- Economic Abuse - controlling money, withholding money, keeping spouse from improving themselves.

- Spiritual Abuse - using scripture or spiritual knowledge to manipulate the other.

The absence of physical or sexual harm does not negate the presence of abuse. In abusive relationships, there is usually a combination of some or all of these categories. Ultimately, all of these forms of abuse result in one individual being reduced in value, emotionally ruined or physically handicapped. For individuals who are physically or sexually abused, it can result in death. Abuse creates a vicious cycle of evil, because children raised in such homes are likely to either become abusers themselves, or get into relationships in which they are abused. Furthermore, children of abusive homes become emotionally wrecked, even if they are not abused themselves. They blame themselves for the abuse, and sometimes take it upon themselves to protect their abused parent. Some have even murdered one parent because of the abuse inflicted on the other parent. Again I must say that abuse is a tool of the enemy that must be dealt with aggressively.

There are some physical and social characteristics that typify the abused wife. She may or may not have been a product of an abusive home. The abused wife takes on certain traits as a result of the abuse. The strongest and most common trait is the intense attachment to her abuser. It is very, very difficult for her to leave him, and many times, even if he leaves her, she believes he will come back. She often has a sense of guilt because she has been made to believe that she deserves or is the cause of the abuse. She is often consumed with improving herself so the abuse will stop. She is often convinced that there is something she must/can do to cause everything to get better. She finds herself making excuses for her husband's behavior. Finally, she does not believe she is being abused. She does not realize that SHE is not the one with the problem. She does not recognize that her spouse will not change without both professional and spiritual help. She does not accept that there is absolutely nothing she can do herself to change her spouse. The Christian wife in this situation has a particularly difficult time because she is trying to balance Christian principles of love, forgiveness and faith, making it even more difficult to recognize when her own life (and her children's) is at stake physically, mentally, socially, economically and spiritually.

The abuser wife has not been studied as well as the abused wife. In my experience, I have seen a variety of characteristics at play depending on the woman involved. Some are pure bullies propelled by the culture of fear they have created in their homes. Her husband and children have learned what not to do in order to preserve peace, so the abusive behavior continues unchallenged. Some abuser wives seek out and marry men they can control. A number of abuser wives have psychological challenges but refuse to get help or acknowledge their need for help. Unlike the abused wife who sometimes takes the hit so her children do not get hurt, the abuser wife tends to care very little about how the children think or feel. Instead she is focused on her own feelings. Some abuser wives are not extreme, but the end result of her behavior is a husband who is controlled and diminished in value. May this not be the impact you have on your husband!

The Old Testament book of Judges records a gruesome case of abuse. It happened at a time when there was no leadership in Israel and each person basically did whatever they thought was right. (Judges 21:25) A Levite man had taken a concubine, but she was unfaithful to him and left him. This man traveled far to her home and persuaded her to return with him. She agreed and they set off to go to the house of the Lord first before returning home. On their journey back, they stopped at Gibeah, a Benjamite city. They felt safe among the people of God, so they rested there, and someone took them into their home. That night, a group of men surrounded the house and demanded that the owner of the house give them the

Levite man so they could have sex with him. The owner of the house refused, but offered to give them his own virgin daughter, and the Levite's concubine. Let us look pick up the biblical account of what happened next from the NIV version of Judges 19:25 - 20:1

"25 But the men would not listen to him. So the man took his concubine and sent her outside to them, and they raped her and abused her throughout the night, and at dawn they let her go. 26 At daybreak the woman went back to the house where her master was staying, fell down at the door and lay there until daylight. 27 When her master got up in the morning and opened the door of the house and stepped out to continue on his way, there lay his concubine, fallen in the doorway of the house, with her hands on the threshold. 28 He said to her, "Get up; let's go." But there was no answer. Then the man put her on his donkey and set out for home. 29 When he reached home, he took a knife and cut up his concubine, limb by limb, into twelve parts and sent them into all the areas of Israel. 30 Everyone who saw it was saying to one another, "Such a thing has never been seen or done, not since the day the Israelites came up out of Egypt. Just imagine! We must do something! So speak up! 20:1 Then all Israel from Dan to Beersheba and from the land of Gilead came together as one and assembled before the Lord in Mizpah." "

What happened next is that the Israelites tried to bring their erring Benjamite brothers to repentance, but they refused and instead came up to fight against them. The first time, the Israelites suffered at the hands of the Benjamites. So they asked God what to do and God not only instructed them to fight against the people who had allowed this evil thing to happen, He also promised them victory. You can read it for yourself in Judges 20:28. When I read this biblical account, I think of the abused wife who is in a 'Christian home'. The Levite reminds me of Jesus and the price he paid for the redemption of this abused wife, who in the story is the concubine. The men of Gibeah remind me of a husband, maybe even a Christian from whom you would expect more. Looking at the Levite's response to her death, I think that although he knew they would sleep with her, he did not think they would abuse her. He entrusted his concubine to them, just as God entrusts his blood-bought daughters to their husbands. The Benjamite men, like many abusers, did not admit any guilt and were even on the defensive. The concubine was dead and could not defend herself. Many abused women are emotionally dead and unable to defend themselves. The Israelites did not take the matter lightly. They gathered as one to seek God, investigate, plan and fight. And God did not hold his own children guiltless of this crime. God sanctioned this family war because He does not handle abuse lightly either. Because of this crime, the Israelites went to war, and lost some of their own. Dealing with abuse is not easy, and sometimes people trying to help get hurt in the process. It was important that the Israelites deal with the issue at stake, even though some lost their lives while addressing this egregious sin.

Sometimes Christians' response to abuse is not as aggressive as it should be. We see the love, kindness, and gentleness in relationships and discard the possibility of abuse. Seeing a couple 'in love' or being a wife who is enjoying those precious times of happiness after being hit does not mean the abuse is over. That is the 'honeymoon phase' of abuse. The abuse will happen again. An abuser has a very serious problem that needs to be dealt with properly. It is not enough to pray for a spouse or couple dealing with abuse and let them go. They must receive knowledge through counseling to adequately deal with abuse, and flee from this great evil. As a physician I have come to realize that if I do not deal with abuse when I see it, my next encounter with that family may be when one of them is brought in dead. If you or someone you know is in an abusive marriage, you must get help because abuse cannot be handled single-handedly. There must be an effective combination of professional, spiritual, and social resources to save the abused, his/her spouse and their children. Anything less than that will result in tragedy. Listed in the Resources section of this book are websites, organizations and literature that can be used to effectively combat abuse.

Endurance

A married, single, widowed, divorced or abused woman has a tough but not impossible task when it comes to marriage. The "O" Factor wife is a strong woman who rises above her own pain to secure a deep relationship with God. Girded with her godly relationship, she gains strength to raise the bar and wisdom to address issues regardless of what her husband does. It takes strength to do what is right when someone else won't do anything, but that is exactly what an "O" Factor wife does. Her choice to live right by her husband does not always depend on him. She understands that living right means loving him and supporting him, but she does not tolerate abuse from him. She adjusts her mindset to see her husband as God sees him. She loves him with a love from God, not based on him. That takes strength. That takes endurance. She takes her cues from her own strong, deep and intimate relationship with God. She keeps her friendship with him even when he doesn't want to do anything. She prays for him incessantly because she is looking for God's intervention, not her own. It takes strength to wait on God, but that is what she does until God gives her an instruction. She waits for that instruction and prefers to stay single if she hasn't received the instruction to marry her dream man. She exercises her faith at all times. She builds up her emotional muscles so she can stand when life is taking a toll on her marriage. Her faith survives if her marriage ends through no fault of her own. Her endurance carries her in the good and bad times before, during, and after her marriage. More than any other chapter, the ladies in the next section exemplify what wives do well and do terribly. Learn from these women, and make your wife hat look good!

Hats off to these wives.

OUR EXAMPLE – The Virtuous Woman

Can I be real? I used to be so happy that this woman was 'fictional' because it was unbearable to think that someone could do all that when I couldn't even get my 2nd grader to school on time without leaving a trail of cinnamon toast crunch all over the house! But then God burst my bubble: she IS real. She is simply the organized Christian woman who puts God and family first. She understands and fulfills all the purpose of God for each stage of her life. Now tell me we can't all do that? We don't all have to go make scarlet clothes for our beds, but we must take care of our homes. We don't have to go plant vineyards. We already have a vineyard: our homes! If God has called you to the workforce as well, then you can and will do that work as well and be blessed as long as you do not ignore your home in the process. The virtuous woman did not do everything in one day. This was her lifetime achievement, the reward of which was a family that praised and appreciated her. Appreciation is not always a big dinner party with gifts and a diamond ring. When your husband says "thank you" or your child says "I love you" or your neighbor says "I like you", you too are a virtuous woman!

OUR EXAMPLE - Abigail

Abigail is an example to us because she had a stubborn husband, but she sailed strong through the ditches of marriage and did what was right. She stepped out and did what she needed to do to protect her household, which included her stubborn husband. She had perfect timing for everything. She knew when to hurry, and she knew when to wait. David described her as a woman with good judgment whose actions had saved the lives of every male in her household. I can't help but wonder - how did she end up with a fool like Nabal? Your guess is as good as mine. But she persisted in being a helpmeet, even to a man who did not deserve it. What an example!

Watch out for these wives.

OUR CAUTION - Job's Wife

Job's wife was really trying to help her husband out of his misery. Things were spinning out of control in their household. They were losing money, lives, and Job's own health and she couldn't take it any more. She could not endure the pain. She encouraged him to forsake his integrity, curse God and die. You know, Job. Just take the easy way out. Maybe for her it was the logical way out. But the bottom line is that it was not God's way out. The only thing that saved her is the fact that Job did not listen to her counsel. Wow. Maybe sometimes it is good when our husbands do not listen to our heart wrenching counsel! She is a caution to us because she was spared. If her husband had listened to her wrong counsel like Ahab and Haman, the husbands of Jezebel and Zaresh who we will be talking about next, maybe she too would have ended up in our warning section.

OUR CAUTION – Sarai

Sarai was tired of waiting for a child. She knew what God said, but maybe, just maybe what God meant was that they could build a family through her servant Hagar. She shared this thought with her husband Abraham, and he agreed, so she gave her maidservant Hagar to him for a couple of nights till Hagar conceived. I've read this story numerous times, but each time I read it, I end up saying to myself, "She did what????? She gave her husband another woman?????" I would have had a hard time with that one even if it was God's will, how much more creating such a situation myself? It was not God's plan for them. Later on, though, Sarai (now called Sarah, the mother of nations) had another piece of advice for Abraham regarding Hagar. This time, her advice was right, and God backed her up. Hagar was sent away, but that was after many years of Sarah having to wake up every morning and see evidence of the bad counsel she gave her husband. Counsel she gave because she couldn't endure.

These women wore the wife hat in all the wrong ways.

OUR WARNING - Jezebel & Zaresh

> These two women, Jezebel and Zaresh, were walking in the complete opposite direction from what a wife should be. They understood that a wife is a helpmeet. They had no problem with that and they actually had husbands who were willing to listen to them. Wow! I know women who would give anything just so their husbands would actually listen to them. So what did Jezebel and Zaresh do with the influence

they had? They counseled their husbands towards evil, not good. We're not talking about the wrong calls we all make every now and then. They urged their husbands to do things that they knew were wrong. Think about that for a second. Your husband may not want a vineyard like Jezebel's husband did, or maybe he is not jealous of Mordecai and trying to kill the Jews like Zaresh's husband. But are there wrong things he desires that you urge him on to get? Like the handicap parking spot he is not supposed to use. Do you say, "Oh just go ahead and park over there honey, it's alright" or do you discourage him from doing what you know is wrong? If you urge your husband to break the laws of the land, don't you realize that sooner or later, he's going to break the laws of God too? Do you know what will happen if he is not the man of integrity that God expects him to be? He will die spiritually, and maybe even physically. Jezebel and Zaresh's evil counsel ultimately led to the death of their husbands.

These women had the "O" Factor!
They wore the wife hat with ENDURANCE.

OUR GOAL - Priscilla

Priscilla is notable above the many good biblical wives. Whenever her husband Aquilla is mentioned, her name comes up too. Many times her name is mentioned first before her husband's. That

105

suggests that a lot about Aquilla had to do with his wife Priscilla. She worked with him at all levels. She was a true helpmeet. First of all she was a tent maker, alongside her husband. This means she must have been physically strong. She knew the scriptures well. In one encounter, Apollos, a learned man with thorough knowledge of the scripture was preaching in Ephesus. The man was incredible! But when Priscilla and Aquilla heard him preach, they decided to bring him home to teach him the way of God more accurately. Priscilla knew the word of God more accurately than Apollos! She must have been spiritually strong in additional to her physical strength. Finally, Priscilla met Paul at a time when she and her husband had been exiled out of Italy. Claudius had ordered all the Jews to leave Rome, so they were forced out of their home and had to move to Corinth. When we first hear about Priscilla, it is soon after this move. We don't find her crying and wanting to go back to Italy. Rather, she embraced the sudden change, stood by her husband, and used her tent-making skills to support her family. She was physically strong, spiritually strong and emotionally strong – a truly strong woman. A woman of endurance!

OUR GOAL - Pilate's Wife

There is no wife who can't relate to Pilate's wife. How many of us have tried to tell our husbands what to do or what not to do? Sometimes we have good reason for our advice, other times we just have a hunch, or a dream like Pilate's wife did. There are some key things to note in how this exemplary wife handled a tough situation. Pilate's wife was a Gentile woman who had come to believe in Jesus. She was a believer with an unbelieving husband, yet she balanced things well. She had walked with her husband for a while. She knew him, and she knew how things worked in the palace. She couldn't go following the disciples; she had a place in the palace! But she still believed. Others were giving their all to follow. She couldn't be like them, but she still believed. When Jesus was brought before Pilate, she had a dream that troubled her. First of all, she was in a position to receive a revelation from God. Secondly, this woman who was most likely Roman, did not blow this revelation off. She knew Jesus was innocent. In a crowd full of people who knew the scriptures, and the promise of a Messiah, amidst the chaos in Jerusalem to kill Jesus and release a thief, there was a Gentile woman who was in place to hear and believe the truth and to act upon it. She sent word to her husband, while he was sitting in the judge's seat! She didn't worry about seeming too forward. The fact that he was ready to rule did not deter her. She didn't just tell him what to do. She presented her case. It went something like this: "I had a terrible dream because of this innocent man. Don't have anything to do with his case." Simple, direct and to the point, and Pilate listened! She was effective because her counsel was birthed out of revelation and she knew how to communicate. Success as a helpmeet comes when your help comes from the Lord.

CHAPTER SIX

THE RIVAL HAT

Who am I competing against? Who am I trying to beat? Whose grass do I find greener than mine? Do these people see me as a competitor or am I fighting against the wind? What kind of battle is it? Is there a third person in my marriage? Is there something I want so badly that it is driving me crazy?

Obaasima Principle: PERSPECTIVE

The key to wearing the rival hat well is to look at yourself in the mirror more times than you look at your rival.

1. Work on yourself and be the best at what you do.

2. Develop healthy habits around your desires.

3. Do not make evil choices in your efforts to be the best.

4. Obtain things through righteous means not devious schemes.

5. Keep a godly perspective

6. Pray. Pray. Pray.

Rivalry is not something we usually pursue, but sooner or later each of us will be made into a rival. You become an executive for one software company, and the executive of the other company becomes your rival. You stand in line before the big race, and suddenly you are a rival to that person next to you. You are Christmas shopping for something and there's only one item left. Suddenly that other woman who is eyeing the same item becomes a rival. Sometimes we struggle intensely for something. We enter rivalry relationships in our efforts to get one thing or to avoid another. Any time you find yourself competing with someone, or wanting what she has, or trying to be better than someone at something, then you and that someone become rivals. Let's delve deeper into some practical examples of rivalry because there are numerous issues in life where we find ourselves in these positions. It could be the quest for a promotion at work, your efforts to have a child, trying to be the best in class, facing another team in sports, the job that keeps your husband away from you, or you could be one of three ladies who all want to marry the only single man at church! There is the TV show your husband watches when you need him to help you. Then there is that word your boss keeps saying is the reason your project can't expand. If you hear that word "budget" one more times, you just might hit someone. How about the struggle with that woman competing for your man's attention and affection? You know her. She smiles at him and scoffs at you, yet your husband can't see through any of it. She could be real, imagined, in magazines or on the internet, but she becomes a rival. And then there is that thing you have worked so hard for yet can't seem to achieve. It drives you nuts when you see others enjoying it when you've worked so hard but still cannot accomplish it. You have become a rival.

How are we supposed to conduct ourselves towards the people who have what we want? How do we relate to people pursuing the same things we are pursuing? How do we relate to the things we can't have no matter how hard we pray? How do we survive the barracuda rivals around us who intend to take us for everything we have? To simply say, "Love them with the love of the Lord" and close the chapter would be silly, because you and I know that in the heat of the moment, we really just want to kill our rivals, don't we? Just reading these examples of rivalry has maybe caused some old emotions to rise to the surface. But listen: there is a purpose and place for the rivalry relationship or God wouldn't allow it. It is a place that is holy and a purpose that keeps us motivated in the midst of the pain. When handled well, rivalry relationships can bring out the best in us. Yes, there is a place for healthy competition and the desire to be the best on the team or to have the highest sales or to get the most compliments about your work. Healthy competition can push us to excel, and many employers use it to motivate their employees. Unfortunately we often don't handle rivalry well so it tends to tear us down and ruin relationships. Trust and security are major foundations for us women in our relationships, but a rival represents neither of those foundations. So we struggle to relate effectively to people we don't trust. Yet God allows us to have rivals and expects us relate well. He permits us to face these tough relationships. He tells us to work hard for something and then we can't seem to get there. How will we thrive in the midst of these rivalries? How will God be glorified through our responses?

If you've ever watched ER or any of the other hospital based TV shows then you may have an idea of what hospital rounds are like. During rounds all the doctors and students hover around a patient and talk about disease. Then the senior physician 'pimps' the junior members of the team with medical questions. The questions are directed to the medical students first and if they don't get it, then the interns, and higher up the ladder. At this point in my career, I have been at every step of the ladder. As a junior team member, I never had a problem admitting my inability to answer the question posed although I was shaking in my pants when I made those confessions! But I would often get irritated when I watched my colleagues trying to make themselves look smart even when they didn't know the answer. One of them would often make up an answer or ask a counter question he already knew the answer to just so he could have something intelligent to say and make himself look good. I would get so upset and frustrated. Sometimes, even though I had the opportunity to help him, I wouldn't. I would be quiet and hope he would fail, but somehow he still managed to impress our superiors. It made me so mad! He was really starting to look better than the rest of us even though he didn't know any more than we did; in fact he probably knew less than others, but the superiors thought he was so smart. I thought about it one day, even rolling my eyes in the process. Then it hit me: there was nothing wrong with him. The problem was that I was jealous! If I would open my mouth and answer a question instead of not wanting to seem too 'forward', maybe I would also be recognized. Maybe if I worked harder and excelled, I would have something intelligent to say and I wouldn't have to struggle. Maybe if I allowed God to work in me the Spirit of excellence, then I would excel above my peers and not become envious of my devious colleagues!! Ouch! Ouch! Ouch! It hurts when God is right, doesn't it? Sometimes the pain of rivalry is not a pain of rivalry per se. It is jealousy! We are upset because that other person has what we want, and we allow ourselves to be consumed with frustration, annoyance and irritation instead of focusing our energies on excelling. Work place rivalry leaves us less productive when we shift out of healthy competition and enter into jealousy. Frustration eats away at creativity. It affects our vision. It alters our perspective.

Ahab did not handle rivalry well at all. Read the story in I Kings 21. Naboth had a field, and not only did Ahab want it, he actually had a vision for it! It was going to be a beautiful vegetable garden, not a vineyard! That's crazy! Think about it from both perspectives. Naboth owns the vineyard; it is his property. He has a vision for producing beautiful grapes. He sits down in the evening to plan for the vineyard, the workers and the best strategies for producing good grapes. On the other side of town, Ahab is also dreaming about the same property but it is no longer a vineyard. He is dreaming of a vegetable garden! Wait a minute: the land isn't his so why is he dreaming about it in the first place? Well, why we choose to be rivals is sometimes a mystery so let's not go there. Naboth didn't ask for a rival, but he got one in Ahab. Ahab was intense about his desire for the property. So when Naboth declined the offer, Ahab sulked and got mad. All Ahab could hear in his mind was, "I want it, I want it, I want it, I want it, I want it, I want it!!!!" So he went whining to his wife Jezebel and with her help Naboth was killed and Ahab got his precious little vegetable garden. He stole it. At the ultimate end of the story, both Ahab and Jezebel were killed too so in reality, nobody got the vineyard.

I want it, I need it, I've gotta have it. Powerful words! We've all been there at some point in life. We tend to get that feeling when we want something that is beyond our reach and we develop an unhealthy craving for it. Yes, it is unhealthy. It's okay to want to win the game, but if your self worth, happiness, contentment, and ultimate fulfillment will be destroyed if you lose the game, then there's a problem. That's the point Ahab got to. His craving for Naboth's property lead him to murder. Our unhealthy cravings have a way of eating at us, our spiritual lives, and our relationships with others. Unhealthy cravings can totally destroy us. Are the things we covet worth the sacrificed friendships and lives? No. So you want a man. That's okay. But what if you don't get one? If your trust and faith will be shattered until you get him then there's a problem. If your desire for marriage has become the basis for your faith then you are off track. Are you praying for healing? Can you stand firm if you don't get healed? If not, then you are at risk to become depressed and despondent. Do you see just how easily a simple desire can turn into an unhealthy craving that turns our focus away from the Lord and only towards what has now become an intense desire? This too is an unhealthy rivalry.

Dealing with **THAT OTHER WOMAN** is the toughest and most painful rivalry position for any woman. Many of us would choose to compete with the TV instead of another woman! This type of rivalry affects self-esteem, creates a sense of guilt and hopelessness, and causes severe damage to the marriage relationship. The sad thing is that it is not uncommon for that 'other woman' to be a Christian too. So let's talk about it. First, let me address you ladies who may have erroneously convinced yourselves that there is nothing wrong with your relationship with that married man. Wake up! It is wrong!!!!! If you don't want to think about it as wrong, then let me appeal to your common sense. First of all, if he can cheat on his wife with you, then he can cheat on you too! And secondly, technically, you are a thief because he doesn't belong to you. You are no different from Ahab. Our society has done a great job of creating grey zones, but God does not abide by these human grey zones. Sometimes we try to sneak the ways of the world into our faith but it does not work that way. Just because everyone else is doing it, that doesn't make it okay. The fact that the pastor is messing around and still preaching doesn't make it okay. Adultery in all its shapes, forms and colors is wrong. Desiring another man when you are married is wrong. Desiring someone else's husband is wrong. Just because you didn't go to bed together doesn't make it okay. That inappropriate touch on the shoulder, the 'brotherly hug', and the well thought out plan to work late together. All of these activities are wrong because another woman's property is being illegally invaded. We make a big deal out of pornography because it is visual. Many women engage in 'imaginary pornography'. Those thoughts and dreams of you and another man are no better than the man who is looking at the centerfold. If you are fooling around with a single man you know you will not marry, that too is an illegal invasion. Pretty harsh, huh? See, God deals with our hearts. Although we like to use that as an excuse, God actually says that the heart of a man is wicked, and if we are honest with ourselves we can agree with that. Don't tell me, after you have made every effort to be alone with the cute pastor at an inappropriate time that your heart was in the right place! Furthermore for you, Christian woman, even the appearance of sin is sin. There should be no dancing around sin. Sooner or later, sin will engulf you if you dance around it. There is no advice except what a mother tells her child when she is walking in dangerous territory: STOP IT!

Now let me talk to a wife who signed up for a marriage of two and now finds herself trying to survive a marriage of three. You might have been the perfect wife, or you might have made a few mistakes, or maybe you messed up royally. Regardless of how it happened, the victim of adultery is in a crucial position. Adultery can have dire consequences. Children on both sides can be affected. Devious schemes can be plotted. In some situations people have contracted HIV and other diseases. Dealing with a rival in your marriage is a spiritual emergency that requires great effort to overcome. You must pray, and you must pray long and hard. It is not optional to sit around and do nothing, or handle it by means of the flesh alone. You need God more than ever before and must do whatever it takes to gain insight and direction from Him. If you do not launch a spiritual attack, you will find yourself falling at the hands of your rival. Sometimes the fall is so great that even if you are delivered from your rival, you are unable to enjoy that deliverance because you have fallen so far away from the Lord and His purpose.

What is prayer, but simply talking to the Lord, crying to him, worshipping him, singing to him, sharing our thoughts with him, AND listening to His voice - the silent voice of prayer, the words of the scripture, the wisdom of the people around us? Prayer is not as difficult as we may make it out to be. The problem is that we don't take it seriously, we don't set aside time for prayer, and once we have prayed, we fail to listen for the Lord's answer. My husband loves to muse over things. It is not unusual for him to answer a question 5 minutes after I have asked the question! I am learning to be patient, and listen for the answer. It is the same way with God. When we pray, it is crucial to listen for the answer throughout the day. It may come through your coworker, a song on the radio, a call from your friend. God answers and gives us direction. Most of the time, we are not listening, or we fail to connect the dots!

If you have a rival in your marriage, do not let a day pass when you have not committed that rivalry to prayer. But start by praying yourself back to life. You must live in the midst of the rivalry. You can't live your life bent on destroying that other woman. Burning her picture might make you feel better, but will do nothing to solve the problem. Going over and cussing her out will relieve some of your anger, but the fire of your anger will rekindle later. Actually it can make the problem worse because someone else will be infuriated! Listen to this and believe it with the depths of your heart: the Lord will never allow anything to happen to you that you cannot bear. You have got to believe this or you will break under the pressure. You may feel broken and rejected, but you are not broken and rejected. Change your perspective and listen to what God says about you. You can handle this. You can bear it. You will come out strong and victorious. Don't turn yourself into a broken woman; that will just become your husband's excuse as to why he claims not to love you any longer. Neither can you spend your life trying to make yourself attractive so he will love you again. No. You must listen to God and choose his perspective of you. You must believe that you are a precious, beautiful princess in the court of your God. Listen to what God says about you first. Then listen to what God will say about that other woman. God has a better solution. God can show you things about her. Through prayer you can command some things into being, and destroy other activities from happening. Only by prayer and submitting to God can you love your husband despite his own foolishness. Sometimes we think our job is to cry, pray and suffer under the circumstances. No. Your task is to pray the truth into being, and ask God for direction on what to do. If God tells you to go talk to that other woman then do it, but you better stay within the boundaries of what He tells you to do.

SURVIVING RIVALRY

In Genesis 37 – 45 we see that Joseph understood the importance of keeping a godly perspective at work. He stayed focused wherever he was and did not fall prey to jealousy and frustration. Early on in life Joseph had to deal with his jealous rival brothers. They couldn't stand that he was Dad's favorite. When he started having dreams of them bowing to him that was it! They sold him into slavery in an attempt to eliminate him as a rival. Joseph was sold and became a slave to Potiphar. He was an excellent slave and was put in charge of all the other workers in the house. Then all hell broke loose and then he had to deal with his boss Potiphar's wife. You could say that Joseph and Potiphar's wife were rivals. Technically they were both trying to gain Potiphar's pleasure but Joseph was serious about serving Potiphar while Potiphar's wife saw nothing wrong with a little sidewalk romance when Potiphar was out of the house. When Joseph refused her advances, she concocted a story and claimed he had tried to rape her. Joseph was thrown in jail but even in the jail he excelled and was put in charge. Think about it. At every level Joseph was the best; with his brothers, in Potiphar's house, and in the jail. He was always excelling and was put in charge of his peers. Joseph was an Israelite slave who was made a boss over Egyptians wherever he went. Can you imagine how annoyed the other workers must have been? Here Joseph was; suffering the pain of being sold by his own brothers, being made a slave, and then being imprisoned for trying to be a good guy! He obeyed his father, helped his brothers and refused to abuse Potiphar's trust. All that righteousness bought him hatred, slavery, a jail cell and numerous rivals. He could have turned despondent or frustrated at his situation or the people around him. Instead, he excelled and rose above his peers.

Daniel had other issues to deal with. A whole book of the Bible is named after him. There was always competitive rivalry drama going on in the palace. The palace rivals were relentless. Daniel's fellow palace workers were so ticked off by him that they created a plot to get him killed and their plot was successful. These guys worked up a plot that was so devious that even the king couldn't help Daniel. He was thrown into the lion's den. Talk about crazy rivalry at its worst. Here was Daniel – a young man taken captive in Babylon, removed from his friends and family, given a new name and put to work for the king against his will. That's enough pain to have to deal with; the last thing you need is a bunch of jealous rivals antagonizing you year after year, king after king. But Daniel survived. He excelled. He maintained his godly perspective at all times. He was the best and the kings he served always honored him above his annoying peers.

When we are hurting, it is very difficult to make right decisions. The position of rivalry is a painful one. The rivalry position of desiring something is particularly difficult when you watch others enjoying your desire, but your prayers for it just don't seem to get answered. It is extremely difficult to remain cheerful and full of faith when your spouse is blatantly cheating on you or is unwilling to make changes for the sake of peace. It hurts when a friend or coworker takes advantage of us or deliberately puts us down. Bridal showers and family gatherings are incredibly tough for the single lady who wants to get married and has prayed her heart out for years. The barren woman may have a tough time going to the store to buy gifts for the new baby at church. All these hurts have a way of making us tough, and sometimes that toughness thickens into a wall that even God is unable to penetrate. In the first chapter, we discussed the center of feelings and desires (the soul) and how to keep the soul lined up with the spirit. All Christians, male or female, must routinely examine themselves. The Bible also says that the people of the world are shrewder than we are. There is no successful company that does not examine itself regularly to determine its strong points and weak points, good decisions and poor decisions, revenues and expenses. There is no successful business woman who doesn't do this for herself either. Why do we as Christian women think we can be successful without evaluating ourselves and making the needed changes and adjustments?

Once we find ourselves in any rivalry position we have to constantly examine ourselves, and realign ourselves with the Lord and with God's Word, or we might sometimes feel like we are losing our minds. I have to do it daily, and even then it takes me weeks to get back on track! Examine each thought, each motive, each action. Be brutal with yourself. Be honest with yourself. Do not give way to pride, which will always try to convince you that you are right and everybody else is out of the will of God! Sometimes you might have to entrust yourself to a stronger lady who will tell you the truth, but you have to be prepared for it! Don't ask for the truth if you can't handle it. It is not an uncommon teaching that if there is sickness, pain or suffering, or even a difficulty, then we must have done something wrong. This is not always true. There is a diversity of spiritual experiences in the Bible and it is important to interpret scripture correctly. How about the scriptures that describe people being wrongly accused? Those who suffered at the hands of evil men? After preparing the way and baptizing many, John the Baptist had his head cut off. Was it because he was in sin, or did he not have enough faith? So our efforts to examine ourselves must focus on truth that redeems us, not hypotheses that leave us even more broken.

Stay focused on your goal. Your goal is to please God. The goal should never be to get back at someone, or to change your spouse or even to get what you have been praying for. The goal is for you at all times and in all situations and circumstances to be in the center of where God wants you to be. You know what Satan's issue with Job was? Very simple. Satan was convinced that Job only served God faithfully for the wealth and protection that he received from God. Satan's position was that if all that was taken away, Job would curse God. Powerful words. Can that be said of you? It can whenever your faith loses its ground because you didn't get what you want. Ouch. I believe that for the Christian, there is an incredible place in the permissive will of God. His permissive will allows some of the painful situations that come our way. He determines the duration and intensity, but we determine the outcome. This is why one of us can have a long bout with cancer and still praise God with her last breath, and yet another loses her faith altogether because she was not healed. The one who is able to stay strong to the end is she who has learned to stay focused on God, and continue trusting him through each painful moment. She has learned to stay connected through prayer and the Word.

The "O" Factor woman understands that being a rival doesn't mean she has to get her evil streak on! Instead of focusing on her rivals, she focuses on herself and her God. She changes her perspective from them and unto herself. She stops looking at the grass on the other side, and inspects her own garden. She finds ways to improve her work. She puts in a little extra time of study. She works hard, like Daniel and Joseph. She prays and keeps focused on what God says about her, her work, her marriage, her commitments and her rivals. Keep this kind of perspective and you'll soon forget about the little tricks your rivals like to play. This principle works in church, at the supermarket, and in the mall. Do not allow yourself to sink because someone else seems to be rising up. Work on your own floats and move your way up! If you have to wear a rival hat, throw some perspective on it and wear it with style!

Hats off to these rivals.

OUR EXAMPLE - Leah & Rachel

These two ladies were scheming and doing all kinds of things to get their husband Jacob's attention and affection. Leah was the not-so-good-looking one who Jacob was tricked into marrying. Rachel was the good looking one who was desired by Jacob. As if this rivalry wasn't enough, God saw that Leah wasn't loved and decided to allow her to have children, while Rachel could not. Later on God opened her womb and she had a child. In between all this drama these two girls were handpicked by God to birth the twelve tribes of Israel! Despite intense rivalry, goodness was birthed. The names of their children and each one's meaning were as follows: Reuben (see a son), Simeon (he that hears), Levi (associated with Him), Judah (praise), Dan (judge), Naphtali (struggle), Gad (a troop), Asher (happiness), Issachar (reward), Zebulun (dwelling), Joseph (fruitful or addition), Benjamin (son of my right hand). In the midst of their rivalry God was working, God was moving, God was building a nation unto Himself. He picked these rivals to do it and they were not so distracted by their rivalry that they did not recognize the significance of each child. They named each child with accuracy. The only exception was Benjamin who was originally named Ben-Oni (son of my sorrow) by Rachel, who gave birth to him as she died. Jacob changed his name appropriately to Benjamin. These men reflected their names and the prophetic words spoken concerning their lives and the tribes that would be birthed out of them. What a legacy these rivals left for us. They were not perfect in how they dealt with things, but they kept the right perspective and accomplished destiny.

Watch out for this rival.

OUR CAUTION - Peninnah

Penninah and Hannah had a bitter rivalry! Peninnah made a career out of making Hannah miserable. It was awful! Year after year, she tormented Hannah just to irritate her. Hannah would weep, and loose her appetite. You might say Peninnah had a reason to keep her guard up. After all, Elkanah loved Hannah more than her. The only thing that gave Peninnah importance was her children! So what was the real issue here? Peninnah was insecure. Her ranting and ravings were simply an expression of her own fear of being knocked off her pedestal. Now the warning here is for Peninnah because one day Hannah got up! **She prayed and cried out to God for change and**

He heard her. He didn't just give Hannah a son, he also made Penninah irrelevant. Peninnah's name is not mentioned ever again! Whatever she was up to, it didn't matter anymore. Even in the pain of rivalry, God will not tolerate evil. Our insecurities are not an excuse for sin. If you choose to be the Penninah in your rivalry situations, one day soon you too will be forgotten.

This woman wore the rival hat in all the wrong ways.

OUR WARNING – Michal

Michal was a rival in more than one way. She was David's first wife and is described as one who loved David. In fact, none of David's other wives are described this way. Later on Michal became the center of rivalry between David and Paltiel (I Samuel 25;44), the man she left David to marry when he was fleeing from Saul. David had her dragged back into the palace when he became king. Michal comes back to the palace to find all these other women already in position and she is thrust into being a rival. And unlike the old days when it was just her and David, now David was a bonafide king with a kingdom of people to care for and she had to share him with these other wives and with the people of Israel. She had rivals and clearly she didn't like it and didn't know how to handle it. David had already had one experience with the ark and it left Uzzah dead. David was determined to do it right the second time. So he spent an entire day dancing before the Lord, making sacrifices to God and blessing the people of Israel. It was an incredible day! And the icing on the cake was that God was pleased and no one died! But all Michal saw was drama, annoyance, and yet another thing her husband was obsessed with instead of being obsessed with her. She was sick and tired of all these people, all these things that David valued over her. So when David came home after this amazing day, she made her disdain known. He came home after an incredible day to find a bitter, disrespectful and annoyed woman waiting for him. She scoffed at his praise, and taunted him for worshipping his God with reckless abandon. She was pissed off and she made it known. She got the weight off her chest, but her actions did not please God. For not knowing how to handle rivalry properly, Michal paid a hefty price. Her husband clearly didn't need her or want her and he made that known to her. She never had children. Barrenness was the ultimate curse for a woman in biblical times. The worst part is that we really never hear much about her again.

These women had the "O" Factor!

They wore the rival hat with PERSPECTIVE.

Shiphrah and Puah the Midwives

These two ladies were exceptional! When God places people, circumstances and situations together, He has one thing in mind: His purpose. There is a purpose for your annoying coworker, the job your best friend got, and the game your team lost. These midwives understood that they were placed together in Egypt for a purpose. Puah did not try to make herself look better than Shiphrah. She did not try to gain the favor of the king at the expense of her coworker. Shiphrah did not blame Puah when the king questioned their actions. No. They feared God, and obeyed Him together, knowing it could cost them their lives. So God was kind to them. He blessed them and gave them families of their own. This is what God will do when we choose to live at peace with our rivals, and pursue two simple things: His purpose, and His pleasure!

CHAPTER SEVEN

THE MISTRESS HAT

Am I leading a team? Do I enjoy leadership?

Who is following me? Do the other girls roll their eyes at me behind my back? Is leadership taking a toll on me?

Obaasima Principle: STRENGTH

The key to wearing the mistress hat well is to be able to handle the pressure

1. Believe in yourself.

2. 'Fess up when you make a mistake, then move on.

3. You are the leader. That is not the time to wear the mother, sister or friend hat.

4. Lead with wisdom.

5. Brace yourself.

In modern times, the word 'mistress' tends to be used in reference to a woman who is having an affair. I know you turned to this chapter to see what juicy advice I was going to give on how to be a good mistress! Stop it! We are not going there! In Bible terms, the word mistress was used to describe women who had slaves. In Genesis 16:9 the slave girl Hagar was told to go back to her mistress Sarah and submit to her. In this chapter, we shall consider the mistress as a woman who functions as a leader. A leader is anyone who has authority, oversight or direction over someone else. This includes bosses, mothers, teachers, division directors and certainly anyone with a secretary! If there is anyone in the world who follows you, takes directions from you or relies on your counsel, then you are a leader aka a mistress! With this precedent in mind, we realize that we all function as leaders at some level, whether we like it or not. Unfortunately, not all of us possess the needed leadership skill or mindset to be effective in this role. The principles of leadership are not reserved for those with the title of a leader. They are available for anyone to live by. If we all carried ourselves as leaders even when we aren't the boss, imagine how far our communities would go! If we identified ourselves as leaders at work even when we aren't the department heads, wouldn't our attitudes be a little different? If we realized that the next-door neighbor is watching how we live, wouldn't we be careful how we conduct ourselves? If we understood that unsaved Uncle Joe is thinking about going to church, why would we sit around the dinner table and complain about our pastor? The CEO (leader) of a company does not badmouth her own company! It is the disgruntled workers who do that. This begs the question: are we disgruntled workers unhappy with our faith/church/life or are we CEOs over the world?

Women have a few unique problems when it comes to leadership. One is the attitudes of others towards women in leadership. Many in our society and also in the church have a hard time taking instructions from a woman and often unconsciously assign high level positions to men. There are countless times in my career that patients have called me a nurse because it didn't even occur to them that I could be their doctor. The spin off of this attitude is that sometimes it is women who have a hard time taking instructions from other women. As leaders, women sometimes fail to take bold steps either from fear or lack of knowledge, and end up setting ourselves up. How many times have you heard a mother say, "You wait till your father gets home!" The good news is that these problems are not insurmountable.

Our goal as mistresses is to lead our followers towards the will of God. As we have come to understand, every single one of us is a leader in some form or fashion. We are all mistresses. It is crucial then that we know how to be effective leaders. The principles of leadership are simple and apply to both the business woman and the mother. Leadership is a broad subject, and this chapter is not an attempt to deal with this subject in its entirety. I would like us to consider specific issues that are crucial to our success as mistresses in our society today.

INTEGRITY

2 Corinthians 8:20 NIV

"For we are taking great pains to do what is right, not only in the eyes of the Lord, but also in the eyes of men."

So do you play by the rules? Do you cut corners? Do you underestimate or overestimate to make the books look better? Do you ever keep money that was supposed to be a donation? How closely do you obey the Bible? Have you ever embellished a story "so your children would understand'? When you're supposed to be somewhere, do you get there on time? What do the people around you say about you? Do people trust what you say or do they need it in writing? These are all issues of integrity.

Integrity is the firm adherence to a standard of living especially when no one is watching. It usually involves moral issues, but is also a principle of life. The nitty gritty of integrity is not found in the hard core rules, but in the seemingly little ones. The rules of life involving respect, trust and truthfulness. For many of these things, there is no immediate consequence. The judge of these matters tends to be the people around us and whether they perceive us as 'good' or 'bad'. Well, there is a judge in these matters. God expects us to play by His rules at all times. Why? Because it doesn't matter how saved we are as leaders. If we lack integrity, the world will not accept our message.

132

Unfortunately, integrity is not abundant among Christians. The lack of it is the primary root of most of the problems we see in church. Whenever we fail to follow the precepts of the Lord in any fashion big or small, we have literally invited the devil to come in and create chaos. The lack of integrity is seen in the pastor who instructs her secretary to tell a caller she is not there. We see it in the treasurer who changes the numbers around by just a few dollars. It's in the mother who tells the children to eat their vegetables while she munches away at her junk food, and in the friend who makes a promise and doesn't live up to it. The people you lead will respect you and follow you wholeheartedly only if they believe in you and trust you as a person.

From this we draw The Mistress' Leadership Principle #1: I must be a woman of integrity. I must obey the Word of God at all times and in all circumstances no matter what is going on. I must recognize that I set an example for the people I lead, and my integrity will win their confidence and trust.

HARD WORK

II Thessalonians 3:8b-9 On the contrary, we worked night and day, laboring and toiling so that we would not be a burden to any of you. We did this, not because we do not have the right to such help, but in order to make ourselves a model for you to follow.

II Timothy 2:10 Therefor I endure everything for the sake of the elect, that they too may obtain the salvation that is in Christ Jesus, with eternal glory

There is a young Olympic athlete who woke up at 4:30AM every morning to exercise and practice before school. She would get home at 9:30PM on school nights because she had gym, practices and meets after school. She got her homework done in between gyms and before bedtime. She was determined as an athlete and worked hard for her goal. She won gold in her sport at the 2000 Olympics.

Leadership is hard work. Let's face it. Some of us don't want to be leaders because we don't want to be bothered, we don't want the hassle and we are (are you ready for this?) lazy! Well, since we are already leaders, the choice is not between being a leader or being a follower. It is between being a good leader and being a bad one. The effective leaders of today are those who work hard, and it is no different for women in the body of Christ. If we want to be successful mistresses, it is going to take some work. If we are going to be effective representatives of Christ to the world, then we need to get our acts together. It will take effort to keep our bodies in shape. It takes commitment and diligence to do the right thing, even though everyone else at work is helping themselves to the company office supplies. It is not easy to have integrity when no one (sometimes even our supervisors) is playing by the rules. Keeping our knowledge up through studying (for school, work or our faith) is crucial and requires effort, especially if you have other responsibilities. This kind of work will not always come with a paycheck, but a good mistress recognizes that effective leadership takes hard work.

Ladies, we need to gird ourselves with strength because we have work to do! We all have so much to do that 24 hours never seems like enough time. But God has given us everything we need for the lives he has called us to. (2 Peter 1:3) A lady recently came to me with a prayer topic and we agreed to pray and come back together the next day and share what the Lord had said. A few minutes into praying I got one of those thunderbolt thoughts: this woman is relying on me to hear the Lord and tell her what to do! I better fast, pray, read the Word, do whatever I need to do to hear Him! I can't get up till I hear Him because she is depending on me. There are people in all of our lives who are depending on us. Our families, friends, students, children, coworkers, neighbors etc. Being a proper influence on them will require effort on our part. I don't know of any other way to work but to work hard. Maybe it is because of my profession. I am often asked how I can stay awake for more than 24 hours straight. When there is a sick child in front of you and that child's life depends on you, you do whatever you need to take care of her. You don't sleep, you don't relax until the child is okay.

The world is in a spiritual state of emergency. We must give ourselves fully to the work the Lord has given us to do if we are going to be successful in our task as mistresses in the kingdom. The Mistress' Leadership Principle #2: I have work to do! There are people who are depending on me to show them the way to the Father. I must work hard unto the Lord, doing my best at all times for Him and for the people He has blessed me with.

DEFINED ROLE AND FUNCTION

There are two mistakes in leadership that guarantee failure. The first is when the leader does not realize that she is the leader. The second is when the followers do not know who the leader is. This might sound too simple to be true but it happens all the time. If you do not see yourself as a leader, you are guaranteed to fail. If you know you're the leader, but don't understand the role you are supposed to play, you're going to have a hard time. We must understand the expectations of us as mothers, teachers and friends. That is part of the purpose of this book. When we have specific responsibilities we must know what is expected of us. This is true for our secular jobs as well as the work we do in church. You have to know what you're supposed to do. Furthermore, you can never forget your role as leader. That means that no matter the kind of relationship we have with the people around us, we must never forget that we are the leaders. This is crucial when we hold specific leadership positions over others. You must not only set an example, but you must set a high standard in faith, conduct, and speech. Nobody wants a leader who is just like them! There is nothing wrong with being friends with the people you lead but you must never forget that you are the leader. And it doesn't matter if it is during office hours or after work, on the phone or at a party, during church service or out on the parking lot. You are always the leader.

How in the world can the followers not know that I'm the leader? Well, that can happen if there is no appointment procedure or if I don't act like a leader! The appointment issue is pertinent only for team leaders and certainly not for friendships and other relationships. If a pastor appoints a leader but there is no official announcement to the affected individuals about their new leader they'll have no way of knowing. Or they'll hear it through the grapevine and that could be dangerous! When I started serving at our church, I was wearing so many hats and I didn't want to have too many titles so I just lived under the blanket title of 'Pastor's Wife' even though I was working in several areas of the church including administration. So when I made certain administrative decisions, the affected people would question my authority to make those decisions. It created chaos, hurt and unnecessary confusion. Once everyone understood that I was the church administrator, attitudes changed. Your followers need to know that you are the leader by official appointment, and it should be punctuated with conduct from you that is befitting of a leader. Your children know that you're their mother, but your actions can reduce their perception of you as leader if you treat them like your peers.

The Mistress' Leadership Principle #3: I must know exactly what I am supposed to do in every leadership position I hold. As a church worker, at my workplace, in my friendships, as a mother. What is expected of me? I can never forget that I am the leader, even during the super bowl party when my team is winning! I must always act like a leader.

BEING UNDER & BEING OVER: UNDERSTANDING AUTHORITY

Matthew 8:9 NIV

"For I myself am a man under authority, with soldiers under me. I tell this one, 'Go,' and he goes; and to that one, 'Come,' and he comes. I say to my servant, 'Do this,' and he does it."

Once we recognize our role as mistresses, it is important to recognize that the role comes with a measure of authority and influence. What I say to my children will impact their lives so I need to get it right the first time around! If I give my husband bad advice, I could lead all of us down the wrong path! Most of the time when leaders get into difficulty with authority, it is because they have gone on a power binge. I think there is a more subtle and probably more prevalent abuse of authority that exists, and that comes from individuals who have authority, but fail to recognize it. Every one of us who fails to recognize our roles as leaders is also abusing our authority. Why? Because there are people following our cue whether we realize it or not. How many parents do you know who have cited their own parents' example as the reason for their own performance as parents, whether good or bad? Our actions and words have an impact on others. You have power over someone's life!

After accepting the fact that you have authority, the next step is to understand how to execute that authority. The single most important way to be a good leader is to be a good follower. None of us is queen and lord over all. We are all under someone else's authority. Our own ability to recognize, respect and obey authority is the key determinant in our ability to execute the authority we have. Recognizing that leaders are also servants to the people we lead will affect your leadership methods. How well do you receive correction? How does it feel when your boss yells at you? Do you follow your pastor's instructions even when you disagree with them? Can you obey your team leader even if she is younger and less experienced than you are? Are you ever afraid to talk to your boss when you have messed up? Do you ask for permission before making certain decisions or do just do whatever you want because, 'I'm in charge'? Experience is not the only way to learn, but in the matter of authority, experience as a good follower is the main lesson. For each responsibility we have, we must understand whose authority we are under. As a wife and mother, it is your husband. As a church worker, it is your team overseer, elder or pastor. As a worker it is your boss. As a friend it is the Lord. It is important to stay under authority at all times.

With the power and influence of authority comes responsibility. The leader is always responsible for the outcome. This is true for good outcomes and bad outcomes, when the 'follower' made the mistake, and even when the leader was not aware of the problem. It always comes back to you, the leader. This should not stop us from making the hard decisions, but it should humble us enough to make sure we know what we are doing! An effective mistress takes responsibility for the actions of the people she oversees. Even if your team members disobey your instructions, it is not the time to blame them and leave them alone to take the hit. If our children's mistakes are a result of our failure to adequately guide them, we need to take responsibility. If our brothers and sisters are in need and we have the ability and opportunity to help, we need to take responsibility. Similarly, when we are under authority ourselves, then someone else takes responsibility for our own actions. You will make many mistakes as a leader. There are times you will face opposition. Have you ever been challenged by a 2 year old? Or your best friend and Christian sister? Has one of your team members ever rolled her eyes at you and probably even called you something I won't mention here? This is why it is important to stay under authority yourself: it keeps you protected during the hard times!

The Mistress' Leadership Principle #4: "I've got the power! Someone will be affected by what I do and say. I must first stay under authority myself, then I will learn what it means to be led and become a good leader myself. Everything that happens on my shift is my responsibility! I need to have accountability for the actions of the people I lead."

PERSEVERANCE

So far we've established several hard facts about leadership

- It isn't easy

- It requires a lot of sacrifice and hard work

- All leaders make mistakes

- All leaders will face opposition

- All leaders must take responsibility.

These 5 facts suggest that there will be many times that you and I will want to quit! You can't quit because your children are adolescents and don't want to follow the Lord. You can't let Satan's attacks stop you from serving God! If you made a mistake, that does not disqualify you as a mistress! If someone criticized and humiliated you that does not mean your life is over! There is no great man or woman (Christian or not) who came into greatness with ease and stride. Each one faced difficult situations, in some instances repeated failure, and opposition. Their ability to persevere through the difficulty is what drove them into greatness!

I believe that God has spent the last few years teaching me to toughen up. I faced a lot of opposition, pain and tears during my first few years as a pastor's wife. At one point, I was so down that I regretted ever getting involved in the ministry or marrying a man called to the ministry. In fact, I even mourned over those decisions. That was a real low point in my life, and thank God that He drew me out of that. There are many other times though that I throw my hands in the air and just want to be left alone. The most common trial is the daily struggle to not take anything personally, to refuse to be hurt, and to love the unlovable. Above all this is to believe and accept that God has called me as a mistress in this time and season, and that neither I nor the people around me can afford to have me quit or do a lousy job. I must keep on keeping on no matter what comes my way. Think about this: if you don't wear a belt, the devil won't know to kick you below it! On the other hand, if the devil knows the kind of trouble you can't bear, he will keep bringing it back till you quit! Make up your mind once and for all, that you are a mistress for life. Accept the fact that hardships will come your way, and learn from each experience God allows you to go through. Each hardship (whether you pass it or fail it) is still an experience that will help you become a better leader.

The Mistress' Leadership Principle #5: I can't give up. I won't give up! God has called me as a mistress. He will give the strength to walk through each challenge, and learn from it. If you want to be an incredible leader and rock that mistress hat, it will take strength. Lots of it!

Hats off to this mistress.

OUR EXAMPLE – Eve

We don't think of Eve as a leader but as the first woman, she was a leader of all women. Unfortunately she often gets a bad rap for the whole fruit and snake saga but I really admire Eve because she demonstrated a vital leadership skill: the ability to survive and thrive when the chips are stacked against you. Picture it: you have messed up, your husband is blaming you, God is mad, and everyone I mean everyone is getting punished! Eve's punishment is that she will bear children with pain and her husband is punished with hard labor. Now imagine the pregnancy with morning sickness and all, and no pregnancy book to tell you what to expect next. Adam is busy dealing with his hard labor, and you live every day wondering if the back pain, vomiting, swollen legs, weird appetite or your bad attitude is the labor God punished you with. And then one day your water breaks. You feel a pain you have never ever felt before. It gets more and more intense till you feel like your abdomen is about to rip open. And it does, sort of, when Cain comes out. That's when Eve says something that explains how she survived. She says "With the help of God I have brought forth a man." All along Eve was going back to her God for help. Yes, she went back to the same God who punished her. She didn't hide from God, she didn't sit in a corner and sulk and she didn't give up on herself. That's a leader.

Watch out for this mistress.

OUR CAUTION - Sarai

Sarai had one thing going for her: God had his hand on her. She didn't always stay under His authority though. In fact, you could say that Sarai got Hagar into a tight spot. Hagar never asked to bear a child for Abraham. The whole thing was Sarai's idea. And when Sarai's seemingly clever plot was done, Sarai had nothing but regret. The wrong she promoted came back and haunted her. Now where are the verses that talk about Sarai praying for Hagar, and being patient with her? I wonder if their absence is a good thing for you and I because many times, in the midst of the pain our followers cause us, we have a hard time reaching out for God. So did Sarai. She found it easier to mistreat Hagar to the point of driving her away. God, in His mercy, dealt with the issue himself, and gave both Hagar and Sarai a second chance. We don't always get that chance.

This woman wore the mistress hat in all the wrong ways.

OUR WARNING - Potiphar's wife

This mistress completely misunderstood what leadership is all about. She thought it gave her the right to take advantage of her workers. She did not realize that sometimes God uses us to groom people who will soon take authority over us! So she tried to lure Joseph, a servant in her home, into bed with her. When that plot didn't work, she went on to tell a lie about Joseph that landed him prison. But

God had a plan for Joseph, and was grooming him for leadership. Before the story ended, it was Joseph who became Pharoah's second-in-command. That gave him authority over Potiphar and his wife! Poor Mrs. Potiphar!

This woman had the "O" Factor!

She wore the mistress hat with STRENGTH!

OUR GOAL - Deborah

Deborah was a great leader. Incredible! Back in her day, ladies didn't just get up and decide to be judges, but when Deborah got the call she rose to the occasion quickly. She had an urgency to go about her Father's business. It was time to go to battle. The enemy was upon them, for crying out loud! But there was just one problem: Deborah was a judge, not a military general! She would have to enlist an army to get this thing going so she called on Barak and gave him the word of the Lord. Barak wasn't so sure and tried to play it safe at a critical time when time was of essence. If I was Deborah, I can't say I would have been so gracious and accommodating of Barak. I might have just let him go and moved on. Not Deborah. She was patient and wise in her leadership. She knew Barak was the man for the job even when he didn't know it. So instead of losing her cool or trying to take the battle into her own hands, she simply made some adjustments, kept him in leadership but provided the oversight and support he needed for success. She gave him some godly insight into the future while she was at it. And yes, they won the battle!

145

146

CHAPTER EIGHT

THE SERVANT HAT

Who do I serve? Who serves me? Is it easy for me to serve or would I rather be served? What is the motive for my service? Am I too proud to serve or am I so proud of who I am that I can serve and not feel devalued?

Obaasima Principle: SELF-WORTH

The key to wearing the servant hat well is to know what you bring to the table. If you don't know who you are, you will despise the unique opportunities you have to serve others and the resulting blessings that will come to you.

1. Don't be too proud to serve someone else

2. Great entrepreneurs and inventors solve other people's problems. They are servants.

3. Service comes out of wisdom and knowledge.

4. Service is always rewarded.

I went to see a dear friend the other day. She was speaking at a huge Christian women's conference. There were women in beautiful pink conference T-shirts all over the place. As I was walking over to see her a woman called out to me. I looked over and there was a group of 7 women sitting on a round couch together with this older woman who was calling out to me. I walked over with a little trepidation. She calmly asked me if I would help her. I said yes, but I felt and looked puzzled because I had no idea what kind of help she needed. She told me she needed me to help her get an even older lady up to the conference room. I happily agreed but quietly wondered if she had asked the other ladies sitting next to her. After all, I was the one without the pink T-shirt and least likely to be attending the conference or be a Christian for that matter! As we walked, she told me of how this older lady had cared for all the rejected and broken people in the church when she was younger. I was so moved by what this woman's life represented! Then she talked of how others often didn't even bother to take care of this matriarch. That's when my jaw dropped, my heart broke and I understood why I had been called to help her; no one else would! I stopped in the middle of that hallway, looked that beautiful old lady in the eye and told her what an honor it was for me to serve her by carrying her bags and helping her get to the conference.

There are so many women in church. There are quite a number of good Christian women too. But there are few great Christian women. Why is that? Greatness comes from serving others but many of us don't have time or energy for servanthood. We are so very busy doing all kinds of things that are good, wonderful and necessary.

Half the time we are so tired that the thought of adding one more task to the to-do list would cause some of us to burst into tears. We are looking for someone to serve us not vice versa! But servanthood is not so much about doing things; it is more of an attitude than an activity. God is not calling us to go out there and serve everyone in the world. What he wants is for his daughters to have the heart of a servant; the willingness and humility to serve others as part of who we are. Like many Christian women all over the world, I work incredibly hard for my family, my husband, my church, my career and my God. In fact, I don't know any other way to work but to work hard. A servant takes this up a notch though. A servant doesn't just work hard; she works hard out of love, honor and obedience to her leader.

Service is not just about church. There is also our places of employment where everyone has to answer to and serve someone. Even the CEO has to service the needs of the board or she is out. No one is an island unto themselves; everyone is expected to serve and solve problems. Everyone is expected to work hard and with good intentions. The team is expected to fulfill a specific mandate. How do you serve at work? Are you a valuable and reliable member of the team? Can your supervisor count on you to do what is expected of you? Are your evaluations times of joy or times of dread?

How about your everyday life? Are you a servant? I gave an example at the beginning of the chapter of how I ended up serving an older lady. Can you think of times in your life when you have served others? Is serving others a natural thing for you, or is it hard to get out of your flow to help others or serve their needs? Is it easy to serve your husband or is it annoying? Is it a pleasure to serve your children or does it drive you crazy? Does your degree impede your ability to serve?

As Christian women, when we serve others we do it out of love, honor and obedience to our master God. We work hard to please Him, not just to work hard. Think about that for a minute. Can you imagine how awful it would be if after busting your chops and working hard God was completely displeased with all the work done and all the sacrifices made? Check out this scripture:

"Not everyone who says to me, 'Lord, Lord', will enter the kingdom of heaven, but only he who does the will of my Father who is in heaven. Many will say to me on that day, 'Lord, Lord, did we not prophesy in your name, and in your name drive out demons and perform many miracles?' Then I will tell them plainly, ' I never knew you. Away from me, you evildoers!'" Matthew 7:21-23 NIV

That is one scary scripture for a hardworking sister like me. I work way too hard to get up there and the good Lord won't even recognize me! We can work incredibly hard doing nice Christian things but may not be doing them for God. We can work hard without having a servant's heart. All that work would be nice but our 'servantless' attitude would not please God. I think this scripture is reminding us that all our hard work has to come from a heart of service to God. We have to do His will and in fact that's what His servants do! We cannot please God without being servants. We cannot be women of God if we are not prepared and willing to think and act as servants of His. The "O" Factor woman lives a life of service because she recognizes her worth and the good she brings to the table. She serves others out of an understanding that she is here on earth to use her gifts and talents to solve problems. She understands that when she does this, she is a blessing to others and incurs great reward from God. Why else should you be employed if not to solve problems? You aren't just a servant; you are a problem solver! So let's glean a little more about servants by looking at specific things a good servant does in the biblical context and then translate it into how we serve others.

'The Lord came and stood there, calling as at the other times, "Samuel! Samuel!" Then Samuel said, "Speak, for your servant is listening." And the Lord said to Samuel......' I Samuel 3:10 NIV

The good servant listens: God called out to Samuel three times, but did not speak to him until Samuel declared he was a listening servant. He wasn't just ready to listen; he was ready to obey what he heard. When you are really ready to listen to God then there is also a readiness to obey His word. The rest of the nation of Israel was in turmoil; no one was seeing or hearing God. But once Samuel learned to be a servant, God wouldn't stop talking to him and he became established as a prophet. The servant of God is always listening for His voice, and still hears from Him even when everything goes haywire. Are you a servant? Are you listening? Are you hearing from God? Are you paying attention? Are you listening to your supervisor? Are you hearing your mother's instructions?

- The good servant listens. We do not serve at our own convenience. We don't just do what we feel like doing. No. We recognize the people we serve – our bosses, our CEOs, our clients etc and we listen to them. By listening, we gain greater access to solutions and add value to our communities.

"A king delights in a wise servant." Proverbs 14:35 NIV
"A wise servant will rule over a disgraceful son, and will share the inheritance as one of the brothers." Proverbs 17:2 NIV

<u>The good servant is recognized and rewarded by her master:</u>
God is looking for servants! His eyes are roaming to and fro around this great earth and he's not looking for buildings or technology or wealth. He is looking for good servants who will do the right thing regardless of circumstance. God recognized good servants like Samuel and Job, and chose to interact with them. The servant may not get instant praise and often gets no praise for prolonged periods of time. Even worse, sometimes servants get abused by the very

people they are serving. The path of a servant is filled with troubles, woes, ridicule and pain but we serve regardless of this because we know that our good work will pay off. Make no mistake: the good servant will be recognized! There is a reward, and sometimes that reward includes promotion to brother-level inheritance! Woohoo!

- The good servant is rewarded. When we adopt the heart of a servant in the work place, in our volunteer work or in any venue where we serve, our work will gain notice, promotion and reward. Many people live in disappointment because they expect reward for their hard work. They expect to be helped by friends and family. They expect applause for living life. The good servant does her job regardless of what others are doing. She does her duty and expects nothing from anybody. She is not a fool. In fact she is the wisest of the lot because she doesn't end up disappointed and broken because of what others may or may not do.

- Instead she walks in contentment and peace, and ultimately enjoys the benefits of her service!

"Whoever serves me must follow me; and where I am, my servant also will be. John 12:26 NIV

The good servant stays close to her master: The good servant is attached to her master. The good servant remains true to her source.

As servants of God we stay close to God and do not stray from His ways. We do not adopt the ways of the world in our efforts to move up the ladder. We do not get confused by success. No! We remain attached to the vine. Our source and life remain rooted in Christ and in the ways of the Word. We do not serve in isolation. We do not live schizophrenic lives that make us sacred in one place and secular in another. No. We stick close to our biblical principles all the time. We stay close to our master. We stay close to the company vision. We align ourselves with the directives of our supervisors.

- The good servant remains ruled by her Christian convictions even at the work place. As we work/serve, we practice the principles of godly living and remain attached to our source. Unless my work as a doctor is rooted in my Christian faith, I cannot profess to be a Christian doctor. If my career is not rooted in God then I am simply a doctor who happens to be a Christian. The same is true for all other career paths. The good servant will stay close to God and His way even in the corporate world.

"Who then is the faithful and wise servant whom the master has put in charge of the servants in his household to give them their food at the proper time? It will be good for that servant whose master finds him doing so when he returns. I tell you the truth, he will put him in charge of all his possessions." Matthew 24:45-47

The good servant is trusted with everything: That verse reminds me of Joseph! A slave in Egypt who is put in charge of everything at Potiphar's house, then he is put in charge while in the prison, then he is put in charge of all of Egypt by Pharaoh! Of note, he was still a slave! Wow! It is the faithful servant, the one who has learned and practiced rank, who does the right thing when she is being watched and when she is not being watched who will be promoted to the top of the chain! That promoted servant understands the purpose of being in charge and continues to do what is right. As a result she is entrusted with much!

- Are you a trusted member of your team? If not check your level of faithful and wise service. This isn't just about promotion, rank or salary. To be entrusted with the wealth of your company means you can be trusted not to steal it, squander it or misuse it. At your performance evaluation, may it be found that you are doing the right thing all the time for the people in your realm of influence, that you gave the food at the proper time so to speak. You took care of your team. You took care of your company. You could be trusted with everything.

'So he (Naaman) turned and went off in a rage. Naaman's servants went to him and said, "My father, if the prophet had told you to do some great thing, would you not have done it? How much more, then, when he tells you, "Wash and be cleansed'! So he went down and dipped himself in the Jordan seven times, as the man of God had told him, and his flesh was restored and became clean like that

of a young boy.'" II Kings 5:13-14.

The good servant looks out for the interests of the people she serves: The nice thing about this story is that it begins with a servant girl who tells Naaman about the prophet who can pray for his healing. Think about it. She didn't have to say anything. She could have kept that information to herself but she shared it so Naaman could be healed. Then he goes over and is told by the prophet to dip in the Jordan seven times for healing but he gets upset and storms off in anger. His servants could have just said, "Okay! Let's go back to Syria!" Instead they had his best interests at heart and convinced him to listen to the prophet so he could get healed. They stuck their necks out for him. The good servant looks out for her mistress. The good servant goes above and beyond. The good servant takes care of her mistress. The good servant looks out for her mistress. She serves her even when it may not be necessary to do so.

- Women need to support other women instead of tearing each other down. So many women would rather serve a man than another woman. It is not always because the lady boss is mean. Instead it is often because we are too selfish to serve, too proud to look out for another woman's interests or too wounded to 'take it' from another woman. On the other hand, the lady boss also needs to serve the people who work for her and do it with joy and respect. They people who work for us are blessed and empowered when we show them that we have their best interests at heart. I am purposeful about greeting and thanking the wonderful women who clean my office. I could not do my job effectively if they didn't do theirs and I am so careful to appreciate them on a daily basis. I am careful to serve them too.

"After a long time the master of those servants returned and settled accounts with them. The man who had received the five talents brought the other five. 'Master,' he said, 'you entrusted me with five talents. See, I have gained five more. ' His master replied, 'Well done, good and faithful servant! You have been faithful with a few things, I will put you in charge of many things. Come and share your master's happiness." Matthew 25:19-21

The good servant is also a good worker: Think of the laziest person you know. Are you particularly impressed when that person comes up to try to help you? Probably not! We tend to respond best to help from hardworking people. If Naaman's wife's servant wasn't good at what she did, Naaman probably wouldn't have listened to her. Think about it. Your service has much greater credibility when your work is excellent. Your service is trusted when your work is of great reputation. You can never be great at service when you are mediocre at working. In the parable in Matthew 25, it is the servant who worked hard with what he was given who was called a faithful servant. The guy who didn't do much was not only called lazy but was removed from service. Ouch!

- What kind of worker are you? Is your work used as an example for others? Are you effective or do you spend hours trying to complete simple tasks? Would your boss miss you if you quit? The "O" Factor woman understands that excellence as a worker is a prerequisite to service. Actually because she is a servant at heart, she doesn't even see excellent work as a prerequisite per se; it is simply part of who she is. She does her work well.

"You are my friends if you do what I command. I no longer call you servants, because a servant does not know his master's business. Instead I have called you friends, for everything that I learned from my Father I have made known to you."
John 15:14 NIV

Jonathan said to his young armor bearer, "Come, let's go over to the outpost of those uncircumcised fellows. Perhaps the Lord will act on our behalf. Nothing can hinder the Lord from saving, whether by many or by few. "Do all that you have in mind," his armor bearer said. "I am with you heart and soul.'" I Samuel 14:6-7 NIV

The good servant becomes the master's friend: I love reading stories about wealth and inheritance being turned over to faithful servants. In some cases nurses and maids were given inheritances worth tens of millions of dollars! This kind of blessing doesn't come just because of good service. It happens when the servant shifts into becoming a friend. It happens when servants and masters have a relationship that goes beyond the work being done. Even the best of servants are quite good at doing what they are told and doing it exactly as they have been told. A friend doesn't just do what they are told. No, a friend uses their knowledge to go above and beyond expectation. A servant-friend knows her master's business and uses that knowledge to do what is needed. She recognizes what is needed for the hour and doesn't need instruction. She wows her mistress by exceeding her expectation. She wows her way into friendship and ends up with an inheritance. Jonathan's servant had such a close relationship with him that his opinion mattered to Jonathan. His agreement and support gave Jonathan the confidence to fight when the rest of the army was chilling.

- Have you shared a joke with your boss lately? Do you have a friendly cordial relationship with your superiors? Do you anticipate needs and take care of them? Do you know the true nature of the company and what is needed to move things to the next level? As a church worker have you graduated to knowing what is needed for the ministry? Do you know your pastoral leadership? Are you a friend of the ministry? Be a servant who approaches service from the perspective of friendship.

In this book, we have talked about the many roles that we play as women. If we gain any insight at all from this book, let it be from this section. Of all the roles we play, being a servant at heart is the most crucial, for if we succeed at this role, we are guaranteed success in all our other roles. When you know the value you bring to the table, it is easy to use your gifts to serve others. It is natural to be a blessing to others because it doesn't take away from who you are. There are so many rewards for the servant. To wear this hat well, you have to have enough confidence in who you are that you can be willing to give up your time and energy for someone else.

Hats off to this servant.

OUR EXAMPLE - Naaman's Wife's Servant

This young lady is not mentioned by name. The Bible says 4 very significant things about her story.

- She was an Israelite, captured during a raid

- She was a servant to the wife of Naaman, the commander of the Syrian army

- She led her master to Elisha so he would be healed of leprosy

- He was healed

Our service to the people around us must make their lives better.

Our work should add value to their lives. We should direct them towards the Lord. This young girl did not ask to be put in the situation she found herself in. She was an Israelite, yet here she was serving these 'Gentiles'. She could have just done her job and prayed for her master. Many of us live our lives like that – just doing our jobs, surviving and saying our bedtime prayers. She could have just done her job and prayed for her own freedom. In fact she could have done an excellent job and simply withheld the information she had about how Elisha could help her master. But she did not. She provided information and her words were even repeated to the King of Syria. Think about it. This servant's words were repeated to the king! This led to a spiral of events that resulted in the healing of her master. She is truly an example to all of us, to serve everyone we come in contact with, irrespective of the circumstances of our relationships with them.

Watch out for this servant.

OUR CAUTION - Hagar

Many times, a good servant is given many benefits and opportunities. A good servant may even be promoted into a place of authority and prominence. When promoted, a servant must never forget that she is still a servant. That is where most of us get it wrong. When in need, we know how to cry out to God. Once promoted, we start acting like we are in charge, and forget that even in our 'promoted' state (better job, new boyfriend, money, or even answered prayer) we are still servants of God. That is the same mistake Hagar made. Her mistress Sarai entrusted her husband to her. (Yeah, I agree with you that was Sarai's mistake, okay?) But see, Hagar didn't really have an issue with Abraham. It was when she conceived a child, a pleasure her mistress had not known, that she began to look down on Sarai. Her actions led Sarai to mistreat her and ultimately Hagar ran away. The angel of God met Hagar and told her to go back and submit to her mistress. In other words, go back to being a servant. Because she obeyed, and because God had promised to make her son Ishmael into a great nation, she was spared the punishment of God and is now a caution to us to never abandon our role as servants.

This woman wore the servant hat in all the wrong ways.

OUR WARNING - The fortune teller

The slave girl was a faithful servant in the sense that she used her 'gift' to serve her masters and bring them great wealth. The problem is that the source of her gift was divination. The reason for her service was evil. Her service was rooted in hell itself, so once Paul cast the evil spirit out of her, she was no longer of use to her masters. The real value of your service will be found in its source. The fortune teller teaches us an important lesson and her story should cause each of us to answer these questions:

- Why do you serve?

- What is the source of your service?

- What value do you bring to your master and where did you get it from?

Be careful. When you serve, make sure your motives are right and your source is pure. If not, one day every impure source will be cut off and you will be left with nothing.

This woman had the "O" Factor!
She wore the servant hat with SELF-WORTH.
OUR GOAL – Ruth

Ruth wore many hats well, but her ability to serve is what made her so good as a daughter, wife, friend, lover, worker, sister, and even when she had to face the rejection of widowhood. Ruth exemplifies all the qualities of the good servant outlined in the chapter above. She listened to instruction and followed it so well that even when Naomi wasn't leading her well, she could see past her bitterness and remain faithful to her. We don't see her play the role of a rival but I imagine there was at least one other woman who had been waiting to be Mrs. Boaz and saw Ruth as the woman who stole her man! Ruth learned to listen to the right voices so she could focus on the one she was called to serve instead of haters around her. Ruth's ability to listen, serve and to be faithful lead her out of pain, mourning and brokenness and into Boaz's arms. But that wasn't it. Even God was so impressed that he broke his own rule just so he could bring this amazing servant into the lineage of Christ! She didn't serve for nothing. Nope. She was greatly rewarded!

CHAPTER NINE

THE LOVER HAT

When was the first time I fell in love? Who would readily say that I love them? How do I love a man? How do I receive love? What is the best way for anyone to tell me they love me? What is the best way for my spouse to tell me he loves me?

Obaasima Principle: TIMING

The key to wearing the lover hat well is to know when it's time to love and which expression of love to exhibit.

1. Is it time to date him?

2. Is it time to make love?

3. Is it time to buy her a car?

4. Is it time kick him out?

5. Is it time to punish her?

6. Is it time to show mercy?

I admit it: I often take sneak peaks into this chapter more than all the others. This is the juiciest chapter of the book! But if you turned to this chapter first, you need to go back and start from the beginning. The reason you must go back to the other parts of this book is that you will only be an effective and sound lover when you are complete in yourself and you are fulfilled as a daughter, sister, friend, wife, mother, rival, worker, mistress and servant. We project ourselves into our relationships, and how we feel in life is going to affect how we love and how we are loved in return. You may have heard it said that women are emotional beings or that we are more in tune with our emotions than men are. I'm not sure about that but there is no question that in general, women 'feel' differently from men, and we certainly love differently too. Unfortunately, our way of loving often gets us in trouble too.

I fell in love when I was in college. He was absolutely wonderful! He was cute, he said everything I wanted to hear. Funny thing is that I can't even remember anything he said except that it sounded really good in my ears! When he called, my heart jumped and I was on cloud 9 for the rest of the day. I lived for that next phone call. I had our future all mapped out. I even knew what he was going to wear at our wedding. The best part about this love story is that the groom was in a different part of the world. He had not asked me to marry him and we weren't even dating! During one of my lovely moments of day dreaming, I decided to have a little Bible study and pray for my groom. Naturally I turned to Song of Songs for a sure word from the Lord. Oh I got a sure word from the Lord all right. He snapped me out of my little soap opera box with these choice words:

Song of Songs 2:7 NIV

"Daughters of Jerusalem, I charge you by the gazelles and by the does of the field: Do not arouse or awaken love until it so desires."

These words appear multiple times: Song of Songs 2:7, 3:5, and 8:4 Thankfully it did not take me long to hear the warning from the Lord. There is a time for love. There is a time to love a man and be loved by him. There is a time for that love to be dormant. When love is dormant, it is not absent. It is simply quiet. Then there is a time for it to be aroused, you know just shaken up a little bit but not in bloom. Sort of like a young couple that ends up breaking up the next week. Even more aroused is an engaged couple who is really in love and yet haven't consummated their love. And then there is a time for it to be awakened and activated, and that's when we just throw ourselves in all the way. With each stage of love comes a different way of expressing love. Think about that for a second. There is a time for love.

There are many different ways to classify the concept of love and its means of expression. The categories of love that have been easy for me to understand are the Greek definitions of love: storge, phileo, agape, and eros. We touched on this briefly earlier, but let's talk about each of these in a little more detail now.

Storge – family love

Storge love is a natural affection that comes with a sense of belonging such as between relatives, a mother and child. Certain levels of friendship can have this kind of love. We will talk about this type of love in the chapter on motherhood so we will not spend too much time on it here. We read in Song of Songs about not arousing love till it desires. Whether or not your child was an Ishmael or an Isaac, once that child comes into the world a desire to love is aroused and you fall in love with that baby. Even when that child behaves like a knucklehead and even when she is being disciplined, there is a love between family members that remains. The expressions of this love can vary and can also be abused. Some parents have abused their children in the name of love. Others have failed to discipline their children at all, also in the name of love. Where is the balance between these two extremes? Mature *storge* love is balanced and knows to express love through both discipline, patience, acts of affection and times of withholding. Mature *storge* love knows when and how to express itself. Part of your task as an "O" Factor woman is to love your family with mature *storge* love. Balanced love. Love that knows when to buy what the child wants and when to let him wait till he can handle it. That mature love that knows to remain patient when the sick relative is having a fit. That mature love that gives just as much restraint as it gives reckless undeserving love, but knows the right timing for each. Family love is necessary for the "O"

Factor woman. We were all born into a family that we are assigned to love. Your task as an "O" Factor woman is to *storge* love them the right way at the right time.

Phileo – brotherly love

Phileo love is a tender affection between two people. It can be between friends, siblings, comrades or mates. You can even express it to a stranger. It is not completely selfless because it requires a response in order for the love to thrive and keep going. It adapts itself based on the response. Think about it. Have you ever had a friend who had a need and you really couldn't help him, but you felt so bad about doing nothing, so you decided to do something? You know that thing you did which you now regret because your friend didn't appreciate it or abused that expression of love? What you had was a *phileo* love and it was bruised when your friend failed to respond appropriately. You regretted your actions because this love requires a positive response to keep it going. *Agape* love, which we will talk about next, does not need to receive anything back. I know this makes agape love sound superior but there is nothing wrong with *phileo* love. I'm actually relieved that it is a type of love because it means I don't have to *agape* love everybody! I can *phileo* love you and it's okay that I don't throw myself all the way in. This is key. Too many of us show *agape* love in situations when *phileo* love is required and then we get upset when we aren't shown *agape* love in return. When you recognize off the bat that you're dealing with *phileo* love then you learn to adapt your love. You don't need to withdraw it completely. You just adapt it and that's okay. The "O" Factor woman knows how to give *phileo* love, and she understands what it takes to maintain it.

Agape

Agape love is completely unselfish, and gives without expecting anything in return. I know we all like to believe we only love our friends with *agape* love. But do you remember that friend you lost? You know, the one you let go because you were the one who was always calling and doing stuff for the friendship? You lost her because you *phileo* loved her. If you *agape* loved her then it wouldn't matter whether she responded or not. Agape love doesn't care what it gets back. *Agape* love is generous. It gives even when it is not deserved. It seems like a lot to ask, because it is, but don't worry about the reality that you and I often fail at this love. The Master of *agape* love is the Lover of your soul, your heavenly Father. This is the kind of love with which He loves us. It gives freely whether you receive it or not and whether you like it or not. It keeps going even when you don't like it. It remains even when you reject it. It is possible for us to love with this kind of love, but we need to be sure we are giving that *agape* love to the right person and for the right reason. There are many times that the "O" Factor woman will give agape love. When you cook yet another meal for that husband who

170

ridiculed the last meal. When you give money to that friend who didn't even thank you for your last gift. When you comfort that child who boldly told you that you weren't his mother. Yes, we will give agape love many times, but we need to be sure that it is the right time to show it otherwise our love will be taken advantage of.

Eros

This kind of love is reserved for your husband. Oh yes, and for no one else. This is a romantic, emotional love which includes physical attraction, sexual desire and sexual fulfillment. When a woman arouses this love prematurely, there is bound to be pain and regret at some point in her relationship. The human reality is that despite our best intentions, we can have sexual desires without having a husband. Sometimes we don't even intentionally arouse it, per se; the guy was just sculptured and fine!! What does a sister do with that? First of all, realize that sexual desire is not the same as eros love. Secondly make a firm decision not to act on the sexual desires outside of marriage. Even when you are married, there will be times of separation when desire will arise but can't be fulfilled with your lover. Thirdly, find something to do so you don't turn your frustrations on some innocent soul who can't meet your needs. Desire is born out of a series of events, some of which are controllable. When one goes from married to single, it doesn't erase your sexual history and sexual desire. You can't do anything about

171

that longing to have sex again. Here is something you can do though. You can control the sequence of events that lead you to dream of one particular man in your arms. Come on! Be honest with me about those aimless times of day-dreaming about that guy with his shirt off! Or the books we read or the sexy movies we watch that simply stoke our desires. When you choose not to fulfill desires outside of marriage, you also have to make a decision not to create or stoke fires that you don't need. True *eros* love must find fulfillment. True *eros* love must be created and stoked. You can't be truly married if you don't desire one another and long to be one. Yes there will be disagreements and fatigue and the hustle and bustle of life that can get in the way of fully expressing *eros* love, but make no mistake: *eros* love must be part and parcel of every real marriage. Unfortunately unmarried couples tend to find more fulfillment in *eros* love than the married couples who are so busy living life that they fail to fully embrace *eros*. The "O" Factor woman understands that there is a time for *eros* love and she guards and guides it appropriately. She controls those things that awaken it prematurely, but when the time is right she encourages everything that promotes her God-given desire for her man.

Let's talk about sex

Okay. Let's take it there because we can't talk about *eros* love without talking about the act of marriage itself. Books have been written about this so we can't even attempt to have the entire conversation in one chapter. *Eros* love is not just about imaginary acts. *Eros* love begins in the emotions but culminates in physical, spiritual and emotional oneness. It is not just about sex; we understand that it is prophecy, a picture of Christ and the church, and the utter fulfillment the body of Christ will find when Jesus Christ returns to marry his bride. Sex is not just a desire fulfilled. It is about complete and utter vulnerability, enjoyment and unity. Do not be satisfied just to have sex. Part of *eros* love is to enjoy your beloved's body and allow yourself to be loved by him. You express this *eros* love physically – the warmth, the wink, the smile, the touch, the hug and the act. When we are sad or angry a common reaction is to withdraw emotionally and physically. But when the foundation of your relationship is right, then when emotions have cooled off you will find that this same *eros* love – the warmth, the coy smile, the touch, the hug and the act can bring healing and restoration. To be a lover, you must learn to give sex. Yes. Sex CAN be given. Yes, it is those times when you are tired or have the "world-famous" headache but your beloved wants you. The lover in you will give the act even though it's the last thing you want to do.

Loving Him

We can't talk about being lovers without delving a little more into how we love our husbands. Marital love is complex. It is a little bit of all the kinds of love because our marital relationship can span everything from friendship to enmity and everything in between. One minute you are madly in love and the next minute you really could just kill him! Yes, that is marital love! Knowing this keeps me patient and humble as a lover. I recognize my own swings as a lover and I recognize his too! Love can grow cold, but I have learned to wait patiently because I know it will heat up again. I've learned to wait for those times when I know love will regain its fullness and fulfillment. Like you wife-lovers, I too made a vow of love to a man. A wonderful guide for this love is found in that famous passage that is quoted at many weddings.

1 Corinthians 13:4-7 (NIV)

⁴ Love is patient, love is kind. It does not envy, it does not boast, it is not proud. ⁵ It is not rude, it is not self-seeking, it is not easily angered, it keeps no record of wrongs. ⁶ Love does not delight in evil but rejoices with the truth. ⁷ It always protects, always trusts, always hopes, always perseveres.

The blueprint for marital love is a combination of *storge, phileo, agape* and *eros* love described in 1 Corinthians. When my blood pressure is going up I remind myself that if I love him I must be patient. Sometimes I try to get cautious with my love. You know those times when you are making a major sacrifice and you have a little doubt? Yes. I get like that sometimes too and I have to remind myself that *agape* love is part of the package. Sometimes I won't get a thank you and I need to be okay with that. When I want to kill him, I repeat over and over again that love is kind. When I could say, "I told you so" I remember that it does not boast. Hmm. Loving is hard, but it's what an "O" Factor wife-lover does. The "O" Factor wife-lover exhibits all 4 at various points in her journey of love for her man.

Expressing Love

So there we have it! We have talked about the categories of love and the characteristics of each one. Now let's talk about the categories of expressing love. The categories that have been of great practical value for me are the 5 love languages, as described by Dr. Gary Chapman is his book, *"The Five Love Languages"* – physical touch, acts of service, words of affirmation, gifts, and quality time. Dr. Chapman talks about how each person has a primary love language, and for anyone (especially a spouse) to love them effectively, they have to express their love to them in that particular language, or they will not feel loved. So if you are one whose language is acts of service, you will feel loved when your spouse does things for you. On the other hand, if your language is physical touch, then you will need hugs and kisses, not just a clean kitchen floor to make you feel loved.

Let's take this a step further. Within each category of love, we can express any one or combination of the 5 love languages. And within each love language, there is a scale. So obviously there is a difference between the loving physical touch between my husband and I, and the loving physical touch between my sons and I. That is the scale.

And I can "phileo-love" my friend Alicia by buying her a gift (gifts), baby-sitting her son (acts of service) or telling her how much I appreciate her friendship (words of affirmation.) So we have here the same type of love, but different ways of expressing it.

Whenever the expression of love is inappropriate, it also constitutes a premature awakening of love. Whenever we give a type of love inappropriately, it also constitutes a premature arousal of love. We awaken the *phileo* love for a friend prematurely when we 'loan' them our rent money. When they are unable to pay it back, the friendship is ruined. We awaken *eros* love for men when it is not time for us to, and we end up in bed with them without even thinking about the consequences. We awaken the *storge* love for a child prematurely by having children we are not ready for. And sometimes we don't even have full understanding of how to love our children. But see, this is how we love as women. As with everything else we do, when we love, we throw ourselves into it and give it our all. Yet the scripture admonishes us not to do that, till love so desires. You have to discern the right times for love.

As I have grown, I have become a very selective lover. Nope I don't just throw it all out there because you are so lovable. The "O" Factor lover puts each relationship in perspective. She adapts her love. She times her love. She scales her love. She rarely completely withholds her love because she has a little bit of *phileo* to give everybody! But when it comes to that man the "O" Factor woman has vowed to love, the rules are a little different. Once he has been approved and selected and vowed to, all bets are off except for one: to love him with her entire body, soul spirit. Yes. He gets it all because the timing is right!

Hats off to this lover.

OUR EXAMPLE – Peter's wife

Whenever my husband comes back from a 2-week trip I have a honey-do list ready for him! So imagine what life was life for Peter's wife. Her honey-do list had to be way longer than mine, and she probably gave up on waiting for Peter and got the stuff done! Except for that time when they stopped by the house to pray for his mother-in-law, Peter was gone for literally 3 years following Jesus all over the place! Before that he spent hours on end out at sea fishing. Yes, Peter was the loudmouthed fisherman who resorted to cursing when he was pushed into a corner after Jesus was captured. Peter was the disciple who always put his foot in his mouth with Jesus so I bet he did the same at home too! Peter's wife survived all the travel, all the trash talk, all his questions and ideas, then the sudden disciple status and his new leadership role at the council of Jerusalem. That is a lot for any wife to handle! This woman must have loved her some Peter to be the quiet bystander and supporter who was always there, who loved Peter in spite of himself, who believed in Jesus too and for that greater good, allowed her husband to go. She understood those words in 1 Corinthians 13 about love being patient. It takes a whole lot of patience to take care of everything at home while your husband travels the world. We never hear much about this woman except when Paul alluded to the fact that he could get a believing wife like Peter's if he so wanted. Simple statement, but it implies that this woman was pretty amazing, and her love for Peter must have been an example to all the apostles on the evangelism trail. I'm sure the message was simple: get a wife like Peter's or don't get a wife at all! What a lover!

Watch out for this lover! Her love was meant for the Lord, and we shouldn't give it to people!

OUR CAUTION – Mary Magdalene John 20

Mary Magdalene loved Jesus recklessly and she had to. Mary Magdalene loved Jesus so much because her many sins were forgiven and that is how we must love him. Only Jesus can cover us with the kind of grace that frees us from what we have done and who we used to be. So because she was so grateful for what Jesus had done, she washed his feet with her tears, and dried them with her hair, and broke open an alabaster box of perfume. Unfortunately many women love people and things the way Mary loved Jesus, not recognizing that that kind of love should only be for Jesus. Can we love our husbands that beautifully? Absolutely! But the thing is that Mary's love was rooted in what Christ had done for her. Love rooted in what was done for us can only be reserved for our Lord and Savior. When we love people out of recognition of our past failures and what those people have done for us, the end result can be abuse. Their past actions become a hook or snare, and it is expected that we love them. Hmm. True *agape* love has no strings attached. Mary Magdalene loved Jesus the right way. She's an example for loving Jesus, but don't love others that way. Don't love others because of what they have done for you or what you used to be.

This woman wore the lover hat in all the wrong ways

OUR WARNING - Sapphira

Sapphira understood the part about being a helpmeet but she forgot that God still expects us to obey his laws. Sapphira and her husband Ananias wanted to do a notable thing. Everyone was selling property and brining the proceeds to the church and they wanted to help too. So they decided to give their money to support the gospel. The sold their land and brought some of the money to Peter. That's honorable isn't it? It wasn't like they gave nothing, but here is the problem. They pretended to bring everything when they were only bringing some of the proceeds. That was dishonest. That is below the standards God sets for his people. So Ananias brought the money to the apostles, but Peter saw right through the lie and called him out on it. Without a prayer or a curse, Ananias fell down and died. Wow! Then came Sapphira. Peter asked her if the amount her husband brought was the full price of the land. He gave her a chance to tell the truth but she decided to support her husband by lying. Supporting our husbands does not free us to lie. Both Sapphira and her husband Ananias lost their lives over this little thing that wasn't a big deal to them, but was a huge thing in the sight of God. Think about it. What do we sacrifice? What are the things that die in our lives when we remain silent about sin? Sapphira literally loved her husband to death. You don't need me to tell you that kind of love was not necessary and is certainly not exemplary.

This woman had the "O" Factor!

She wore the lover hat with TIMING.

OUR GOAL – The Beloved in Song of Solomon

The Beloved was not just a passive recipient of love. She was an active player in this love affair and one who adored her lover. Her poems about him and descriptions of him give insight into her utter love and admiration for him. I feel so convicted when I read Song of Solomon because my wedding vows to my wonderful husband were not that juicy and full of admiration and love for a man who truly loves my socks off. There are many women who are blessed to have men who really love them and would do anything for them. These guys are trying their best and would do anything for their wives, but their ladies are not satisfied. Not so with the Beloved. She was adored by her lover and she loved him back with everything in her. She loved the right man and she loved him really well, with no inhibitions. What a love! What a lover! When you find that true love and he puts a ring on it, learn a thing or two from the Beloved. Love him back. Love him back really well!

CHAPTER TEN

THE MOTHER HAT

Am I ready to be a Mom? Have I embraced my role?

Are my children driving me nuts? Can I remain their Mom regardless of their behavior? Can I endure the pain of motherhood? Are my labor pains killing me? Who are my children?

Obaasima Principle: VISION

The key to wearing the mother hat well is to see beyond now. Vision is the foundation of a mother's love.

1. Who are you called to? Who must you raise?

2. What do you see when you look at each of your children?

3. What are their strengths and weaknesses?

4. Who needs some tough love? Who needs a warm embrace?

5. What needs to be developed in your children?

Today I was filled with love, pride and appreciation for one of my spiritual daughters. Whenever I thought of her, a smile crept up on my face. Finally I sent her a text telling her how proud I was of her.

She responded and said something that made me laugh, cry and rejoice. She said, "Thank you for always standing by my stubborn self." Yup, she had been a tough cookie through the years but it made no difference to how much I loved and cared for her. I laughed, cried and rejoiced because it made me think of the joys and pains of motherhood, and the dynamics of the mother-child relationship. Have you ever had a child who you loved so much that it hurt? That child who listens but doesn't always do what you say and you love her anyway? That child whose pain is your pain but you can't do anything about it. You just have to watch and pray. That child who vanishes for a season and then comes back again. You love him whether you see him or not. You rejoice when he comes and you miss him when he is gone. That child who goes against everything you have taught her but your heart aches for her. The child who dies and leaves you heartbroken and searching for answers. The child who rejects your motherhood but you still hold on and love him anyway. Motherhood is full of joy yet it is also full of pain.

You could be a biological mother birthing raising natural sons and daughters. That means that from day one you are on diaper duty, homework call, college expenses and all. Maybe you are a spiritual mother with sons and daughters who look to you for direction and instruction. You might not change their diapers in the natural, but you still carry them emotionally and birth their destinies through your counsel and prayer. There are also the corporate mothers who are raising a generation of career-minded sons and daughters who can excel in specific fields of expertise. They come to you with some skills but after working with you they gain even more. They might call you a mentor and not a mom, but you surely are a mother to them. Any capacity in which you bring something to life in another person constitutes motherhood. What you do for them is an element of birthing. It is labor. It is a bringing forth of a new nature, character or ability. That's motherhood.

Motherhood is made of a lot of things. Motherhood = Love + Patience + Endurance + Faith + Strength + More Love + Amnesia + Sight + Labor + Muscle + Carrying Capacity + Strength + Teaching + Guiding + Counseling + Homework Assistance + Kindness + Hope + Forgiveness + Joy + Wisdom + Pain + Instruction + Laughter + Messiness + Cleaning + Bleach + Extra Kids + Animals of all kinds who need love and care + Kids' Homework that end up being assignments for Mom because the 5 year old can't possibly do an experiment + More Bleach + other tasks as they pop up unscheduled and invade a mother's day.

All these and more form the life of a mother but there is one thing that every mother needs in order to survive the diverse postures of motherhood. That one thing is the "O" Factor motherhood principle of vision. An effective mother does what she does because she has a vision for her relationship with that child. First of all she sees herself as a mother to that child. Without a vision of her own status as the child's mother, nothing will flow out of her towards him. She has to self-identify and embrace her role as mother. This is true of biological children as well. Have you ever wondered how it is that some women abandon their children or fail to care for them? This happens when a woman does not self-identify as a mother; the vital source of a child's life. An amazing concept of breast milk is that it is based on demand and supply. Mother has to keep putting the child to breast and more milk will begin to flow. The ability to produce milk is there, but the process of production begins with mother recognizing the child as hers and stopping everything else to give that child her milk. The more she feeds him, the more her milk supply increases. That's when it flows out of her. To be a mother you must recognize that the child you birthed in the natural needs you. You must recognize that the young woman who keeps smiling at you and listening to everything you say is looking to you to be her spiritual mother. You must agree that the young man begging for attention and help is looking to be molded and shaped into a stronger man. Besides recognizing these needs you have to accept the responsibility. Then and only then will something begin to flow out of you towards those children. The first level of vision is for a woman to see herself as that child's mother. Secondly, she has to see something in the child. The mother has to see potential regardless of whether the child sees it or not. She has to believe that there is something of value in that child that she has to nurture. She has to see beyond that children's current ability and make an investment.

186

She has to see something that is worth her time, money and effort. She needs a vision. A mother works with that vision. By that vision a mother forgives. Because of the vision mother keeps loving the wayward child. Through that vision she finds strength to keep going. Because of vision she overlooks the child's own foolishness and presses on. She produces in each child according to vision. She molds each one according to that good thing she sees. When a mother sees nothing in her child, she leaves him to his own ways. Sometimes a mother sees potential but lacks the ability to birth that particular thing all by herself. Some children don't make it but many others survive. They find other mothers to fill the gap and complete the job.

Before I ever had any biological children of my own someone started calling me Mom. To tell you the truth, it felt a little weird. I was a young inexperienced pastor's wife. I was overwhelmed with all the responsibilities that come with church. I was trying my best but I had people telling me what a horrible job I was doing. I knew I had potential but I could also see my faults quite clearly. Truth be told I was my own worst critic. I had goals, dreams and aspirations. Being a Mom one day was somewhere on that list but I needed help. I needed someone to show me how to do this pastor's wife thing. I needed a mother for myself and yet here comes this young lady calling me Mom. It caught me by surprise. I didn't feel ready or able to take on this task. But regardless of how unfit I felt, she kept calling me Mom. Soon I changed from the "you talking to me?"

response when I heard her say, "Mom?" to turning around and saying "Yes baby?" I was ready to answer to her call and meet her need. Before I knew it, I was transformed from a woman to a mother and I didn't even need an epidural! In another encounter I came across a young lady who desperately needed guidance. She was so broken and my heart went out to her. She had her own biological mother but she needed more help and direction. I took on the task and started pouring into her life. She became like one of my own. I went all out for this one, giving my time, money, advice and whatever it took to help this child. I made myself a mother. One young man asked me to be a mother to him and to mentor him. I sized him up, tested him, approved him and then agreed to the task. Another one called me Mom at a time when many people called me Mom, including people who didn't necessarily consider me to be a mother to them. So I responded with respect but didn't take it too seriously. But she kept coming back for prayer, for counsel, for advice. She stuck close no matter what. Then she did something that warranted a rebuke. That's when many people get pissed off and say, "I don't need you! You're not my mother!" but she didn't. In fact she stuck even closer after the rebuke. Like a biological child who doesn't stop being your child when he gets in trouble, this one refused to let a rebuke end our relationship. She proved her status as a child and by so doing affirmed my role as her mother. And then there are those 3 boys I gave birth to with 3 beautiful epidurals. The last one was the sweetest childbirth of them all because I didn't feel a single thing! I had to be told to push and on the second push out popped a baby boy! His birth was so awesome, but pregnancy was a nightmare. I withered physically and emotionally because of that child I was carrying. It took a toll on me and I know they say you forget all that when the child pops out but I still remember! In spite of all the trauma, I will be the first to admit that it was worth it.

Through pain, requests, persistence and tests it dawns on us and we finally see and accept our roles as mothers. It can begin with a child calling on you. It can start with you seeing yourself as a mother. It can be an adoption process where you check each other out and prove a commitment to each other. It can be because the child just won't go away and you finally give up and agree to be Mom. All these life occurrences and more can open your eyes so you see yourself as a mother. Once you actually see yourself as a mother, then you have to step into the role effectively and specifically. It's not enough just to do what your mother did to you. No. You have to develop a strategy to mother each child. This is why I am not quick to take on anyone and everyone who calls me Mom. There are a specific few who I am assigned to for a season of time to nurture, develop, encourage, direct and challenge in a way that is necessary for them at that time. There are some children who have their arms open wide and eat up everything mother says and does, and there are also those who will be nurtured but only on their terms. They all need a Mom. They all need to be nurtured in different ways. Motherhood strategies are not one size fits all.

Vision for a child comes by looking, listening, feeling and waiting. I spend a lot of time in my biological children's rooms. I've done it since they were infants and I'm still at it even now that they are grown men. I also capture moments on the stairs, in the kitchen, in the car or anywhere so long as the moment is right to search below the surface. So I've been on the floor, in the tent, curled up on the bed, at the desk and all. These are always precious times of bonding and a chance for me to get to know my boys a little better. It's during those times that I find out that what I thought I knew was completely off base, or that my inclinations were right on the money! It's mostly about trying to 'get' my guys; trying to figure out what it is that they really want and are striving for. My best intentions at raising them will be unsuccessful if it doesn't gel with their own intentions so we've got to work together. I've got to know his fears to know his goals and help him figure out the fears to avoid and the fears to face. We've got to be on the same page about college and careers or it is not worth the thousands of dollars. Sometimes I have to open their eyes to the talents and abilities that they haven't even recognized themselves. When you look at and listen to that child, what do you see and hear? What are his talents? What are her dreams? What is his body habitus? Does she have potential in sports? Modeling? What does he want to do but is terrible at? What is he hoping for in life? What does she love to do? What is she good at? What is she striving for? Is she struggling with her identity and in need of affirmation and encouragement? He wanted to be a sailor ten years ago but what does he want now? What has life taught him along the way? Should I challenge him to go to sea or is it truly time for him to move on? To gain vision we have to look and listen to our children. We have to spend time with them and get to know them. We have to feel them out so we can hear the unspoken words and see beyond the natural. Sometimes you feel out a situation and even though you don't have all the facts, you can 'see' enough to know that it's time to back off. I will never forget the time that one of my wonderful kiddos gave me a scare. I went to pick him up from school and found him with his teacher who handed him over to me and pretty much said she was doing me a favor by not taking him to the principal and getting him suspended. I asked what he had done and was told he had tried to choke another kid!!! What??!!!?!!? My boy? I was shocked but I wasn't angry. I knew my boy well enough to know that there was much more to this story. I couldn't get a word out of him because he was crying and out of control. For the next two days all he did was cry when I brought up the subject. I asked if he had choked the kid by accident or if he was angry and he kept answering, "No." So I'm wondering why in the world he would try to choke this kid. Without vision I would have been livid and dishing out punishments but I knew this child too well. There was no way he would choke another child even if he was angry. I knew something else about him: his eyes would dart when he was lying and there was no darting action going on so I knew he was telling the truth. He always internalized his emotions so I knew it was impossible for him to choke another kid.

191

In fact he was so traumatized by the whole thing that I worried that maybe he was the one who had been choked and was being bullied into silence. On day 3 of getting nowhere it dawned on me to stop asking him questions. Instead I asked him to reenact the scene and show me what happened. What I learned changed everything. This is what happened. My son, who was a hug-loving, gentle, 3rd grade giant, was hugging his friend from behind. Another kid called them and they turned around but my big kid got his arms caught around his friend's neck when he turned around. That kid ran off and told the teacher about an alleged choking incident. Wow! My son wasn't a choker after all! I was so grateful that I believed what I had seen in my son and gave him a chance regardless of what the witnesses said. Point is simple: we need vision and we get it by watching our children and paying attention to what we see.

The other element of vision is the concept of visioning. Visioning is a process of getting someone to see what we see. In parenting it has to do with getting our children to see the potential we see. I'm not talking about parents who control their children and force the poor kids to live the parent's dreams. No. I'm talking about when by vision we see something amazing that needs to be nurtured into maturity. Sometimes the child sees it too and allows the parent to mold them. Or the child has her own ideas of how to nurture it. Other times the child just flat out rejects it. This is particularly difficult if dealing with an older child who thinks they know it all, or a stubborn younger child who simply opposes every suggestion you make. This is when visioning is tricky, difficult and painful. The keys to visioning an unwilling child are patience and love. A true mother needs to be able to patiently wait for her child to get it. Children can take a while to come to their senses. In fact some spend a lifetime discovering themselves and finally come to terms with what Mama said years before. Unfortunately some never even get there. Those are hard years of motherhood as you sit back and watch potential being wasted away. This is where patience needs wisdom. A mother needs to use wisdom to figure out how to instill the vision in her child. The child who trusts your judgment will just do it wholeheartedly. Others trust your judgment but they need a little more before it will truly become their own. They might need to see it for themselves. This means Mom has to figure out a way to have the concept modeled out for her child. It might involve a trip so he can see it in action. Another child just needs to hear it from someone else they can listen to, like a successful younger person they look up to. This other child might need gentle reminders of what they need to do to attain the dream. Mom needs to keep coming back with words, encouragements, instructions, and mandates to steer the child along. Sometimes things get to a critical point where a mother has to turn up the heat. I will admit it! I have used a few good threats to get my kids going in the right direction at critical points in time! Each stage, situation, vision and season requires levels of wisdom. Mom has to use wisdom to figure out how best to steer her child in the right direction. Sometimes mother does everything she could

193

possibly do and with all the wisdom and ability she could muster but the child doesn't listen. That's when patience and wisdom need the overshadowing protection of a mother's love. A mother allows her love for her daughter to overwhelm the pain that daughter is causing her. A mother taps into her own love for her child when the child offers up no love for his Mom. A mother practices tough love all the time. The love that doesn't just give the child what he wants because of guilt. It doesn't do what the child should have done just to take care of it. No. It's a tough love that gives the child what she needs even if she rebels against it. A mother goes back to vision: that day when she accepted the call to raise that child. A mother goes back to recognizing that she can't make her child do anything. Her child has to take responsibility. Vision, love and patience keep a mother going and hopeful that her child will finally get it one day. All children have their stints of rebellion. A son can run in the opposite direction just to get away from you. Your mentee can play hard to get and just not take your calls. Your spiritual daughter can just vanish from your life because she doesn't want to hear it from you. Sometimes the child pushes it all the way to the edge. I know children who end up in jail before they realize it is time to turn their lives around. Unfortunately they still have to live out the consequences of their wrongdoing and carry all the burdens that prison life entails. Other children die in rebellion and never turn their lives around. And yet still some eventually get it because Mom won't quit building the vision in them. They finally begin to rise to the task and embrace the vision.

The Biblical book of Proverbs is a book of wisdom and sound instruction. In terms of parenting, one verse sticks out with such intense wisdom - Proverbs 22:6. The Amplified version reads: *Train up a child in the way he should go [and in keeping with his individual gift or bent], and when he is old he will not depart from it.* There is a way in which a child should go. There is also a way in which a child should not go. We are admonished as parents to direct them in the necessary path. We are further admonished that the necessary path is in keeping with each child's unique talents and abilities. Every child has a natural gift. Each child is structured with innate capabilities and abilities that are unique. The "O" Factor Mother looks to see this natural inclination in the children given to her. She leads them by vision. Her first vision is for herself. The "O' Factor Mother sees herself as a mother whether she has biological children or not. She recognizes her own natural abilities as a man with a womb! She is able to bring forth and raise others. She knows that she has something to offer the next generation and she confidently rises to the task. The "O" Factor Mother identifies the children assigned to her and pours herself into them. She considers their lives and sees beyond natural limits. She uses wisdom, patience and tough love to mold each child according to his or her natural inclination. She doesn't abandon her children even when they abandon her. Her heart is big enough to handle the hurt. She doesn't give up hope for her children. She keeps doing what has to be done. She is Mom. She is an "O" Factor Mother. She wears the mother hat with vision!

Hats off to this mother!

OUR EXAMPLE - Naomi

The book of Ruth begins with the story of Elimelech and Naomi, and how they moved to the land of Moab with their sons. After a while, their sons married and life was good until Elimelech and both of his sons died. Naomi was left without a husband and without her children. She lost her motherhood status, so to speak. But there was a young Moabitess woman, Ruth, Naomi's daughter-in-law. And Ruth wouldn't go away. She left her own mother, and father, her family and her country to be with Naomi at the lowest point of both their lives. Naomi was hurting and was in pain, but there was a young woman who needed her and so Naomi chose to be a mother again. Even when she had no child of her own, Naomi remained a mother. Even when she was going through her own pain, Naomi remained a mother. Even though they looked a little odd together, Naomi remained a mother. Even when Naomi wanted to be left alone, she embraced a young woman and mothered her. And through her motherhood, both Ruth and Naomi laughed again. Through Naomi's vision and motherhood, Ruth married Boaz and became part of the lineage of Jesus. Through her motherhood, their dream came to pass. That's what makes her an exemplary mother.

Watch out for this mother.

OUR CAUTION - Hagar

Sarai had waited years and years to have a child. But nothing was happening. Even after God promised her husband Abram that it would happen. So Sarai devised a plan: how about I give my servant Hagar to my husband for a couple of nights? Then she could bear a child for me. After all, that was the way to have a child when you were barren. So she gave Hagar to Abram and indeed, she got pregnant. When Hagar saw that she was pregnant, she despised her mistress who was barren. In other words, she started to have an attitude with Sarai. I have always imagined that Hagar must have tried to get away with her household duties, claiming to have morning sickness and adding that Sarai couldn't possibly understand what she was going through. First of all, motherhood is not a game or a prize or a status symbol and that was Hagar's mistake. Mind you, her mistress was Sarai, a woman God had been called to be the mother of nations. So Hagar was walking a fine line, and Sarai was not going to have it. So Sarai tormented Hagar till she ran away. But God had mercy on her. The angel of the Lord found her, and told her to go back and submit to her mistress. She got a second chance. Hagar misunderstood how and why she was blessed to be pregnant, so she misused the gift she had been given. She is a caution to us because like Hagar, so many mothers forget that we have been given a gift and a heavenly responsibility, not a status symbol. May He show us mercy when we fall, as he showed mercy to Hagar.

This woman wore the mother hat in all the wrong ways.

OUR WARNING - Herodias

Herodias was in a tight spot. She had been married to Philip, but was now married to his brother Herod, the king. With royalty and all that involved, her hope was that her life would go smoothly. But it didn't. John the Baptist would not stop speaking against their marriage. She thought her husband would take care of the problem, but all he did was put the man in jail. She despised him too much to leave him in jail. She wanted him dead. She couldn't stop thinking about it, not even at her husband's birthday party. Her husband, the king, was in good spirits as he watched her daughter dance at the party. So he offered her an incredible gift. He offered to give her anything she wanted, up to half his kingdom. The possibilities were seemingly boundless. She could ask for almost anything: money for dance lessons, a secure future, or even half the kingdom! So she went to her mother for advice, and Herodias saw her opportunity. Rather than doing what a woman with vision would do and secure her child's future, she used her child for her own evil purposes. She prompted her daughter to ask for the head of John the Baptist. She incited her daughter to request for the death of the forerunner of

Jesus Christ. It's one thing to make a mistake when parenting. It's another to do your best to teach and your child still chooses not walk in the ways of the Lord. But when a mother urges her child to do wrong and promotes the murder of another human being, then she has lost the core value of motherhood.

This woman had the "O" Factor!
She wore the mother hat with VISION.
OUR GOAL – Jochebed Moses' mother Exodus 2:1-10

This woman had vision. She recognized something about her child. He was fine. Not just in the physical sense. There was something about him. She couldn't just give him up to be thrown into the Nile and die. So she kept him. She hid him. She kept him safe. And when she could not hide him any longer, she prepared him for a journey and let him sail along the bank of the Nile. He landed in the princess' arms and became her son. His mother was called upon to nurse him at a time when Pharoah was having all the Hebrew baby boys killed. Yet God allowed her son to live, and she was being paid to nurse him! But the time came for her to give him back to the princess. She even had to let the princess name the boy and take him as her own. But he was no ordinary child. He was a fine child. He would soon become a prince of Egypt. A Hebrew boy living right under Pharoah's nose? God must be up to something. But that didn't surprise her, because she knew he was a fine child. Moses' mother put her vision of Moses' destiny ahead of her own feelings of motherhood. She let go of her own desires and needs so this child could walk in whatever calling God had for him. So when she had the opportunity, she kept him. And when it was time, she let him go, knowing that God was still in control. That is what makes her a heroine.

CHAPTER ELEVEN

THE REJECTED HAT

Who rejected me? What was it over? Who am I rejecting? What is stopping me from taking this hat off? Why am I so hurt? Who have I empowered to leave me in this broken state?

Obaasima Principle: PURPOSE

The key to wearing the rejected hat well is to know your purpose and walk in it in spite of the rejection. The ultimate key is to believe your purpose enough to take the rejected hat off!

1. What is your worth?

2. Are you carrying seeds of worth or seeds of rejection?

3. Why are you here on earth?

4. Who can stop you besides you?

5. Are you pursuing you purpose in spite of rejection or because of rejection or regardless of rejection?

6. Does rejection have any bearing on your pursuit of purpose?

Just about everyone has a sob story about being rejected. None of us fits perfectly everywhere and while that is actually a good thing, it leaves some of us hurt because we want so badly to be accepted. We tend to have this innate need to be part of something, or to be accepted or applauded by someone else. Rejection only happens when we don't fit into something we really want to fit into. It is only when we don't get that affirmation we want from specific individuals or groups that we feel rejected. When we don't have a need for that affirmation, then rejection doesn't impact us in any way. So for me being denied access to the NASA tryout program wouldn't bother me one bit because I'm afraid of heights and tight spaces, so you couldn't pay me to go to space! I wouldn't even care if you didn't let me into the NASA simulation lab! My son told me that if I ever went to space, my stomach would turn inside out and he is right! Being denied access to NASA would make me feel relieved, not rejected! If some random guy called me unattractive I wouldn't give a hoot because his opinion is irrelevant. But if I was denied access to the pastor's club that I really want to be part of? Now that would hurt! If my students purposefully didn't list me as one of their teachers that would make me feel rejected. If my husband thought I was unattractive it would hurt big time! Rejection is not just about being denied something. It only happens when we experience hurt from being denied something we really desire.

Rejection is an overwhelming sense of loss caused by exclusion from an experience, a place or a relationship. Rejection is not just the exclusion; it is the sense of loss that comes with it. That sense of loss often happens because the exclusion often implies that someone else is better than we are and is preferred over us. It reminds us that we don't measure up no matter how hard we tried to be the best. It is made even worse when someone else who appears to be less deserving or capable is enjoying what we want. That's when rejection looks us in the face and tells us all our hard work was in vain. For many of us that is very hard to shake off and keep moving especially if we invested a lot into that dream. Rejection often leaves us telling ourselves that we don't measure up and are no good. That kind of thinking is paralyzing and causes us to deny ourselves from the things we are actually good at! The pain of rejection can be as painful as physical injury! I guess there is a reason we call relational rejection a broken heart.

Let's take it a little further. Sometimes we feel hurt by a perception of rejection that isn't real. You know how that goes! You thought for the longest time that this girl didn't like you because of how she looked at you. Then later on you found out she really did like you, she just looked so serious because she had issues of her own! But until you knew the real reason, you walked around feeling pain whenever she came around you. A perception of rejection can be powerful even when it isn't true. Feeling rejected is a strong state of mind; in fact one could say that it is a stronghold. If allowed, it takes over our sense of worth and erodes away our confidence. It weighs on us and pushes us into a corner. Yes, rejection is a hat, but it is a hat that is not pretty. Truth be told, it gets quite ugly sometimes.

Sometimes we feel rejected indirectly because of decisions made by people we care about. Your best friend moves across the country. You are an introvert and you know she loves you but it hurts that she left you all alone. Or your husband sticks to his plan to hang out with the guys even though you have told him you want him to stay home and spend time with you. In reality he loves you and values time with you, but needs his time with the guys. You know that, but you still feel rejected. No matter what you think about Bruce Jenner's decision to become Kaitlin, have you ever imagined how hard all of this must have been on Chris Jenner?

And then there is also institutional rejection. That army sergeant who returns home from war and realizes that she has to fight to survive. She is often left feeling abandoned and rejected by the nation she served. That is the plight of some sections of society; people who for one reason or another feel abandoned by their nation or by a system. That person in jail who was wrongly convicted and has no hope of freedom despite their innocence. I can't imagine a greater pain that that; being held in jail while innocent. How do you survive that? How do you not feel rejected by the justice system, by law enforcement, or by God?

Just the other day a friend and I were talking about old times and reminiscing over breakthroughs, blessings and great things happening in our other friends' lives. My friend gleefully burst out "Favor!" and I said, "Amen!" but inside of me was deep pain. Inside

I was asking God, "What about me? I need your favor." That pain curled into a huge ball in my chest that resulted in hours of true pain, tears and anguish. I felt abandoned by God; rejected by Him even. How come everyone else seemed to be having favor for dinner and I couldn't even get it as an appetizer? Yup, I felt rejected by God.

The stories are numerous, the situations diverse but the outcome is the same: pain. From the little girl who didn't make it in the beauty pageant, to the girl whose boyfriend left her for another, to the woman who was passed over for promotion. Just when I think I've heard the worst rejection story, another one comes along that trumps the last one! There was a woman who was conned into sleeping with a guy then he turned around and rejected her. Then the woman who gave up her savings to help her friend and then that 'friend' accused her of stealing from her. How about that scene in Tyler Perry's *Diary of a Mad Black Woman*? It was particularly awful because Helen, the character played by Kimberly Elise, had invested so much into making her husband a successful lawyer and tried her best to be a supportive wife, but all she got back was jabs of rejection. And then comes that scene. That scene when she discovers that her beloved husband has found another woman and fathered children with her. She discovers this the night she sat up waiting for him on their anniversary. If that wasn't painful enough, he confronts her with his new girlfriend in tow and then drags her out of the house and literally throws her out! That might be movie drama to some, but to many others that has actually been a real life rejection experience.

The pain of rejection can take many forms. It leaves its victims broken and wounded. Some feel stupid for all the good invested and the time lost. Others feel worthless and undeserving of their true desires in life so they settle for less. That sense of being undeserving even manifests when the best is being offered. The rejected one feels so bad that she can't even accept it. So she gets the man of her dreams but she feels so undeserving that she cannot forget the past and enjoy this new life with him. The painful emotions can be pervasive and draining. It causes some to restrict themselves. Others swing in the other direction and overcompensate. Like the young girl who is rejected by the boy she loves so she makes herself readily available to all and becomes famous and desired for all the wrong reasons. She knows the guys just want her body, but being desired by somebody is much more tolerable than the deep sense of rejection she feels. Some become bitter and lose their smiles. They become reclusive and walled in. It also manifests in faithlessness. The rejected girl doesn't believe good things will actually happen to her. She has taken on the role of rejected and doesn't expect to experience good. She might be smiling and laughing but on the inside she feels deep pain. She might love God but inside she is not so sure He will bless her. She has learned to guard herself from expecting anything so the pain doesn't get any worse.

So we have established the reality of rejection, the reasons for the pain and its manifestations but more important than that is figuring out how people survive rejection? J.K. Rowling is the author of the international best-selling Harry Potter books. She is one of the wealthiest women in England but she wasn't always! Her first attempt at publishing the Harry Potter books was met with rejection not once or twice but twelve good times! Many people would have stopped at the fifth rejection, most definitely after the tenth one. How did she find the strength to keep going after being told no over and over again? Publisher after publisher said no until a small publisher Bloomsbury agreed to publish her book but advised her to keep her job as a teacher. The publisher had no guarantee that this book would become immensely successful, but I believe J. K. Rowling knew all along that her book was a good product. Stop and think about that for a second: She survived rejection because she was convinced her book was good. She knew she was a good writer. She was so sure of it that she wouldn't stop writing and seeking publication despite rejection. In so doing she illustrates two key factors in surviving rejection. The first is that you must believe in yourself. You cannot abdicate your sense of self-worth to another. When you believe in yourself no one can make you feel rejected, in fact one could say that rejection only begins when we stop believing in ourselves. Yes our feelings get hurt and we mourn what we can't have, but when we believe in ourselves we don't become rejected. We soon wipe our tears and keep moving because we don't need to dig too far down to know that we can make it. Second thing that Ms. Rowling shows us is that we must find what we are good at and stay in our lane. She taught and did other things she had to do to keep up with her needs, but she kept it real and continued to write. She knew what she was good at and didn't switch to modeling. She stayed in her lane and kept going even when it looked impossible. This was also a manifestation of her belief in herself.

There is also the late Nelson Mandela who was imprisoned from 1964 to 1990 for fighting against apartheid. 18 of his prison years were spent at Robben Island doing hard labor. He was made to sleep on the floor, had a bucket for a toilet and was allowed just one visitor per year. During those years his mother and eldest son died but he was not allowed to attend their funerals. He spent a lot of time in solitary confinement, an effort meant to crush even the strongest person. In solitary confinement one is left only with one's mind and it is our own minds that often talk us into a state of rejection. But despite these harsh conditions, Mandela did not succumb to a state of rejection. No. He maintained his wisdom, charm and self-discipline. He never gave up the fight against apartheid but his defiance was noteworthy and worthy of respect. There were conditional offers of release which he and his comrades refused. They did not take the easy way out of prison if it would cost them their cause. He took time to learn Afrikaans so he could study and anticipate the actions of his oppressors. He remained a leader to other leaders and eventually even won over some of the guards who had been his oppressors. Eventually Mandela was released and later became president of South Africa. How did Mandela survive undeserved hardship and harsh labor? When he became president how did he stop himself from oppressing those who had caused him much pain? Mandela credits *Invictus*, a poem by William Ernest Henley, as being an inspiration to him while in prison. It reads:

Out of the night that covers me
Black as the pit from pole to pole
I thank whatever gods may be
For my unconquerable soul

In the fell clutch of circumstance
I have not winced nor cried aloud
Under the bludgeonings of chance
My head is bloody, but not bowed

Beyond this place of wrath and tears
Looms but the Horror of the shade
And yet the menace of the years
Finds and shall find me unafraid

It matters not how strait the gate
How charged with punishment the scroll,
I am the master of my fate,
I am the captain of my soul.

This poem was written on a scrap of paper that he kept in his cell. I can only assume that he read this every day and remained focused on those words. Those words must have rung true in his mind over and over again. Even in the longest periods of solitary confinement he

209

must have heard repeatedly, *"I am the master of my fate, I am the captain of my soul."* To survive rejection, Nelson Mandela focused and meditated upon a truth that would keep him strong. By this strength he would survive rejection and not become enslaved by it. He was rejected by men, but he refused to be characterized by rejection.

The Bible tells the story of Tamar, the daughter-in-law of Jacob's son Judah. Her story is sandwiched somewhere in between the chapters outlining Joseph's life in slavery and prison. Tamar was married to Judah's firstborn son Er but for some reason he was described as being wicked in the eyes of the Lord so God killed him. As was their custom, Judah had his son Onan become Tamar's husband to have children for his older brother Er. But Onan had no desire to have children who would not be his so he practiced his own form of birth control and would not let her become pregnant. God didn't like that and so Onan was also killed by God. Judah saw a pattern of death among his sons married to Tamar so rather than give his youngest son Shelah to Tamar, he concocted a lie and told her to go live with her father until Shelah was old enough for marriage. However he had no intention of giving Shelah to her. So Tamar lived as a rejected widow in her father's house with no child and no husband. She knew Shelah was old enough at this point and it was clear that she had been rejected and made out to be as a husband killer. Meanwhile Judah lost his wife too and eventually went wandering around looking for adventure. That is when Tamar took off the hat of rejection and concocted a plan of her own that would launch her into the lineage of David. You've heard that adage "Don't get mad, get even!" Tamar's wisdom was way beyond getting even. Rejected women who aim at getting even only buy for themselves more hurt and pain. Tamar refused to sit back clothed in widowhood when had a right to a husband. She heard that her father-in-law was heading to Timnah so she took off her widow's garments, dressed herself up nicely and covered up with a veil, and positioned herself on the road to Timnah. She must have known Judah very well because her plot worked and he was drawn to her. He propositioned her but my girl Tamar wasn't just in this for sex or a child. Her plot went much further than that. She wanted her dignity to be restored! So she agreed to sleep with him but only if he left a pledge for payment. She picked the pledge by which all would know that it was Judah who had slept with her. She picked his signet, his cord and his staff. So months down the line when Tamar was found to be pregnant, accused of adultery, and sentenced to be burned, she confessed to adultery. She even offered up the man who committed adultery with her and pulled out her evidence. How brilliant! Judah instantly confessed to double-crossing her and pronounced her being as more righteous than he was.

The "O" Factor woman understands that she doesn't have to live a life of depression and pain because of what she has been through. She listens to the lessons from J.K. Rowling, Nelson Mandela and Tamar. First of all she believes in herself and knows her strength. She does not sit back and let others define her! She is quite stubborn about this. She looks at herself in the mirror and tells herself who she really is: strong, beautiful, desired, able, witty, and smart! She defines herself as good and walks in that goodness. Like Nelson Mandela, she focuses and meditates on the truth. She doesn't waste time replaying bad words over and over to herself. Instead she

211

repeats the truth to herself over and over again. An Obaasima doesn't shrink back in defeat just because someone told her to sit back and just be a widow! No! She rises up and figures a way out of calamity. She uses what she has to secure her way out! The "O" Factor woman knows her worth and refuses to be stopped by anybody or anything. Even when she is feeling hurt, she still pursues her destiny. She does not pursue a hurt-driven agenda. She focuses on her God-given agenda, regardless of her hurt. Like Joseph in prison and David in the cave, she keeps pushing forward even when it hurts.

You can tell yourself you are great, but it is the Word of God that backs your greatness and gives you purpose. The power is in the Word and that has to be the basis for your belief in yourself. Meditate on scriptures that empower you; scriptures that fuel you with strength and hope and speak to your purpose on earth. Write them on index cards. Listen to the scriptures. Read the Word again and again. Believe what the Word says about you regardless of your natural circumstances. Meditation means looking at it again and again and again until it enters into your spirit. Write it not just on a paper or on your cell phone, but write it on the tablet of your heart. And if you have been wounded and rejected then do the best thing you can do for yourself: be like Tamar, get up and take the rejection hat off! Refuse to wallow in widowhood because a Judah in your life has sentenced you illegally and made you into something you are not supposed to be. Some of us are in pain because we hold that rejection like an accessory. We hold on to it, use it as an excuse and define our lives by it. That just isn't right! One of the key aspects of truly righteous people is that we don't stay down. The Amplified Version of Proverbs 24:16 reads *For a righteous man falls seven times and rises again, but the wicked are overthrown by calamity.* We are not overthrown by calamity or trouble or rejection. We feel the pinch and we cry. But when we fall or fail or are oppressed or make a mistake or go through any kind of difficulty in life we don't just stay down. No! We get back up again. You may have been forced to wear the hat of rejection, but listen to this. You were created with a purpose. Your DNA does not allow you to remain rejected. Connect with your DNA. Get up and take that rejection hat off! Live again!

Hats off to this rejected woman.

OUR EXAMPLE - The widow

This woman had already lived through rejection. As a widow, she had no place in society and no one to fight for her. And then there was this adversary who had treated her unfairly so she went to court. Even there she couldn't find justice so she went to the judge but even the judge told her he couldn't help her. With all the rejection she had already been through it wouldn't have been too surprising if she had just packed up, said, "woe is me", called it a day and gone home. Not this widow woman! Rejection didn't stop her. It almost seemed as if it empowered her! She kept going back to the judge, and back to the judge and back to the judge till the judge figured it out: if I don't help this woman she is going to weary me! He was right! She had already decided that rejection wasn't going to change her resolve, wasn't going to define her and certainly wasn't going to stop her. What an amazing woman!

Watch out for this rejected woman.

OUR CAUTION – Tamar the daughter of King David

Tamar was abused and rejected. Her half-brother desired her so badly that he raped her. What an awful thing for a man to do and for any woman to have to experience! Rape renders a woman powerless and leaves her stripped physically and emotionally. Not only was she stripped by the rape itself, what happened afterwards was even worse. When he was done, he hated her and rejected her as a woman. The last we hear about Tamar is that she was left desolate in her brother Absalom's house. It was not her fault that she ended up living in depression and pain. The pain of her experience became too much to bear because the hat of rejection is too heavy to wear. Tamar was still the King's daughter; she had a right to royalty regardless of what was done to her. We don't know the end of her story, but I hope and pray that she took that rejected hat off and replaced it with her princess crown!

This woman wore the rejected hat in all the wrong ways.

OUR WARNING - Potiphar's wife

Yes, Potiphar's wife is back in the bad hat category! I really wish the Bible told us more about her because I hope she got it right later on in life. She handled leadership wrongly, but she handled rejection even worse. She was in love with Joseph but her love was a pure *eros* kind of love. All she wanted was to have sex with him but he would not relent despite many attempts. Then one day she thought she had

Chapter Eleven: The Rejected Hat

him. There was no way he would say no, but he rejected her yet again. She couldn't handle the rejection, or the even bigger rejection that would come if she had to explain to her husband why she had Joseph's shirt! So she made up a lie that landed Joseph in prison. When our feelings of rejection lead us to lie, scheme, and destroy other people's lives we are left as bitter and forgotten women. Especially when God is on the side of the person who rejected us! We never hear of her again, but we certainly hear about Joseph because he was right to reject her advances!

This woman had the "O" factor!

She 'wore' the rejected hat with PURPOSE

OUR GOAL - Tamar

Who else can be our true heroine but Tamar whose story was told earlier in this chapter. There is a time to be obedient and do what you are told. But sanctions of rejection, emotional pain and mental torture are not worthy of an "Amen". To that we say, "NO" like Tamar did. She devised a plot of freedom for herself and the generations yet to be born. Tamar wore this hat exceptionally well because she took it off! Yes! This hat looks the best when it is not on your head! If you want to look pretty when you have been rejected, then do yourself a favor: Know your purpose and take that rejected hat off!

215

CHAPTER TWELVE

THE BELOVED HAT

Who loves me? How does his love make me feel? What will I do to secure that love? Does my sense of happiness and self-worth depend on that love? Do I use this love for self-gain?

Obaasima Principle: BOUNDARIES

The key to wearing the beloved hat well is to maintain necessary boundaries no matter how loved you are.

1. Are you taking unfair advantage of this love?

2. Is it time to date him?

3. Will this love cause you to make sacrifices you shouldn't be making?

4. Is your destiny compromised by this love?

5. How can you be loved and adored without letting that sweet love be your source of legitimacy?

Back in the 1980s there was a funny sitcom on television in the USA called Family Matters. The sitcom centered around the Winslow family. One of the beloved characters of the show was their teenage neighbor called Steve Urkel. Steve was madly in love with Laura Winslow. He would do anything for Laura and vowed to win her love. Steve was kind, genuine, and sweet. There was no doubt that he adored Laura and would never let anything hurt her. Sounds wonderful for Laura to have been so beloved, doesn't it? The problem is that Steve spoke with a shrill voice, was not particularly handsome and was so very annoying! Laura wanted nothing to do with Steve despite his efforts to woo her. Being so beloved by Steve wasn't enough for Laura to be in a romantic relationship with him. She parked their relationship at friendship and never took advantage of the situation, no matter what Steve was willing to do. Years later the smart, charming and handsome Stephan Urkel showed up and fell in love with Laura. Laura was smitten. All Stephan had to do was wink and Laura's knees would melt! She gleefully fell in love with him and the rest was history. Laura was loved by two very different guys and she had two very different responses to being beloved. How could that be?

Being loved is wonderful and exhilarating but only if you are loved by the right kind of guy! I heard a comedian tell a joke about how ladies file restraining orders when guys like him visit them at work, but the same ladies call it sweet and romantic when Brad Pitt shows up! So true. Your response to being loved will depend on the person who loves you, and the level of wisdom you carry as a beloved. Keep in mind we are talking about you being beloved and men who absolutely adore you. This is a real stack of love being dished out to you, not just lust and not a one-time fling. I am talking about those times when a guy truly falls in love with you for whatever his reason might be and you find yourself in the position of being loved.

There are five kinds of men who could fall in love with you in this world: the infatuated stalker, the sweet guy you just don't want to be with, the okay guy you tolerate and make yourself love, the good man who is easy for you to love, and the man of your dream(s). Each of these gentlemen warrants a unique response to maintain appropriate boundaries for the beloved position you find yourself in.

1. The infatuated stalker

This is the guy who insists on being with you even though you say no. He keeps coming back and invades your life without your permission. The encounters could be sweet and seemingly benign or deeply intrusive. You might find him waiting outside your house. He sends flowers to you at work even though you have told him not to send any gifts. He reads about you online and follows you on social media so he is able to glean intimate details. He could even go as far as to access your letters or email. He could be that old boyfriend who is still as immature as can be. Or that co-worker who keeps giving you compliments about your body but there is a no-dating policy at work. There's also that guy who says nothing but you know all he wants is sex and you are too vulnerable for a superficial relationship. How about that married man you are counseling but you know you are falling in love with him? And then there is the complete stranger who got your picture from a mutual friend and now he just won't go away. This usually crosses the bridge and delves into more of an obsession than true love.

A guy could be cute, rich, famous or say all the right words but if his presence in your life is inappropriate and he keeps coming back then he is what I call a stalker. If the People Magazine man of the year shows up at my doorstep holding roses and looking for me, I will thank him and remind him gently that I am a married woman so his sweet gesture is not in good taste. If he shows up again, then I'm sorry he just isn't cute anymore. He is a stalker in my book and he needs to go! Because the stalker can be wonderful and charming, he has the ability to draw you into an inappropriate relationship if you don't have a strong NO.

The "O" Factor Woman knows who she is. She recognizes what works for her and what doesn't. She guards her life, her goals, her dreams and her visions. When she spots 'inappropriate' coming her way, she nips it in the bud, especially when she realizes that the gestures are no longer cute. A stalker should not be tolerated because he truly will make that inch you give him a mile. The invasive stalker could require a restraining order. Gifts from Mr. Cuteness may need to be returned. Niceties may have to come to an end so he knows your no is a real strong no. The boundary must be clear and in bold!

2. The sweet guy you just don't want to be with

Many women are beloved by this kind of a guy at some point in time. He is really sweet, kind and gentle. He is madly in love with you and would do anything for you. He is not necessarily great-looking; someone might call him average or at worst not good-looking at all. He isn't a stalker because he respects your boundaries and doesn't invade your space. He is so adoring and loving but no matter what he does, you just aren't interested. Your friends try to convince you to just go ahead and be with him because he will be faithful and will take care of you but you just can't do it. Your mother comes over and tells you he would make a wonderful son-in-law and all but begs you to just say yes to him, but even Mom's words aren't enough. No matter who says what, you just aren't attracted to him and have no desire to be with him.

Steve Urkel was that sweet guy who would do anything for Laura but she just didn't want to be with him. All Laura had to do was blink and Steve would be ready to do whatever she wanted. Now that seems like a blessing in disguise, doesn't it? To have a guy at your beck and call willing to do anything for you! So Laura had an opportunity to get a little something out of this inconvenience. She could totally take advantage of the situation and milk Steve for as much as she could get. Why not? She told him she didn't want to be with him but he offered his help so there was no harm, right? Wrong!! Laura chose to treat Steve with respect. She never took advantage of Steve's love for her.

The "O" Factor woman is not selfish and callous. She does not delight in taking advantage of others. She recognizes that being loved and adored is wonderful, but also that it is even more wonderful when the beloved has the same affection for her lover. The "O" Factor woman is flattered that someone adores her, but she doesn't allow that adoration to transform her into a maniac. She does not ask him to do things for her; she asks her friends. She recognizes that the friendship she has with the sweet guy is different from her other friendships. So she doesn't reveal her secret needs to him knowing that he will try to meet them. No. The "O" Factor woman knows that nothing is free and that whatever she asks of him will have to be paid back somehow. Sometimes the sweet guy pays the debt himself with his broken heart. So she keeps the line marked in the sand. She keeps a clear boundary. She does not blurry the lines with false hope for him and a debt for herself.

The stalker needs a strong boundary that he doesn't cross. Your "no" must be a strong one that keeps him out of your life. There is also a necessary boundary when dealing with the sweet guy whose love you will not return. However this boundary is not for him; it is for you. You are the one who must not cross the line. You are the one who must be careful not to step into inappropriate territories. You are the one who must say, "no" to yourself and refuse to take advantage of his love.

3. The okay guy you tolerate and could make yourself love

This guy has some of the qualities on your list but not all. When he opens up to you about his love for you your initial reaction is "no" but it is a weak one. He knows that all he has to do is work harder and he could draw you into loving him back. You know that too and you secretly admire him while wishing he had some other qualities you desire. He makes a decent living but is not insanely rich. He is not the greatest-looking guy but he is okay. His look would work for the Christmas picture! He snorts when he laughs and it drives you nuts, but he never fails to open the car door for you and make sure you are safe when climbing even a single step. That was something your ex-boyfriend never did. He covers you with his coat if he sees you so much as shiver. He watches you but not in the eerie way the stalker does. His look is kind, loving and attentive and as much as you say "no" you can't deny that you want to be with him. With each act of kindness, he draws you in a little more and your heart begins to melt. Have you ever met a guy who you initially were not attracted to physically but you end up developing an emotional connection that confronts your "no"? This is that guy and this is the point when you end up having to make a very important decision.

Every woman should some absolutely necessary qualities that she doesn't compromise on. For me, those absolute must-haves included faith, good-looks and some umph!!! There was no way I could be with a spine-less dude. I can be feisty, difficult and strong so I need a guy who will match me up there and can catch me when I go too far. His strength would manifest in his work ethic, his ability to carry the load, his swag and his unwavering integrity even in the face of difficulty. My man would have to be strong. The other thing is that I always wanted to be able to gaze at my love while he slept so he just had to be cute and nice to look at. I had some preferences but the color, skin tone and nationality weren't important so long as I would simply enjoy just looking at him. Call me vain, but I couldn't compromise on that one! And faith was the biggest requirement of them all for me. He had to be a genuine man of faith, not the fake pranksters who fill the pews but have no real love for God. With those three in place I knew I could tolerate weird jokes, snores and other annoyances but that wasn't all. I could now take the time to look for the finer details of his life, character and goals and decide if I could live with that or not. If you don't know what you want and you aren't clear about what you don't want, then deciding what to do with the okay guy will be tough! Many okay guys showed up at my doorstep, but only a few had all three of my must-haves when they knocked on my door. I needed those three before I could even put in the effort to look further.

You can't create boundaries when you have no idea what the limits are. No one is perfect, but you know yourself better than anyone. You know what you need, you know what you can tolerate, you know what you will regret, and you know what you can and cannot handle at various points in your life. When dealing with the okay guy you need either a strong "no" or a strong "yes". Saying no is actually the easier of the two. It could mean that you know what you want and this guy just isn't it. On the other hand it could be easier only because you don't want to deal with some other realities that are making you say no. Some other things that have more to do with you than they have to do with this okay guy. It could be that you are afraid. You don't want to fall in love. You are afraid of getting hurt. Or maybe you are going for a nonexistent perfection. Which is it and why did you say no to the okay guy? What is it that you are looking for? Is it realistic or is it a fantasy? Why won't you let yourself be loved?

The harder thing to do is to say "yes" when everything isn't perfect. This is the deal: once you make the decision to love a man back, you can have no regrets. You have got to make it work or one day you will look back and have regrets that you cannot erase. When the "O" Factor woman encounters this okay guy and decides to love him, she puts the hat on in full swing and moves forward. If she doesn't find him cute, she decides he is cute. If he doesn't have a lot of money, she decides he makes enough. If his laugh gets on her nerves, she chooses to pick her battles. Once the "O" Factor woman says "yes" to the okay guy, she willingly pushes the boundary outwards and expands her own love and adoration of him. She allows his love to draw out the best of her own love back to him. By so doing, she makes him into the man of her dreams.

4. The good man who is easy for you to love

Many of you have been with this man or you are with him right now. You waited and sifted out the first 3 kinds of guys. This one is not necessarily the one you dreamed about but you love him just the same. He's more than just alright; you really do love him and you actually like him. Initially maybe you didn't know him well and it took a while to truly fall in love and want him. So once you realized you really did like him, why exactly did you play hard to get? Why did you pretend not to like him? Or maybe you were the opposite. You had been watching him for a while and were already madly in love. You were just waiting for him to ask you out and as soon as he did, you were ready to walk down the aisle or if that wasn't on the agenda then spending the night was okay for you. Whew! Slow down sister! There is a nice balance between giving it all up easily and playing hard to get when you are the beloved of the good man you love. The "O" Factor Woman cherishes the good man. She is honest about her feelings but keeps necessary boundaries in place.

5. The man of your dreams

I admit it. I love stories about Prince Charming! In my best stories the prince marries a girl who isn't royalty but because he loves her, he is willing to give it all up for her. A rich, handsome, and famous man may be the man of our dreams and some ladies are blessed to be loved by men who embody all of their dreams! But the truth is

226

you often don't get all the dreams in one. You might get one but not the other. You get a guy who is stupendously rich, but is not particularly good-looking. You don't mind how he looks because you love how he makes you feel with the gifts, the first-class tickets and all the attention you get. That's a man of your dream and you don't want to lose him or his money. Or the guy who is tender, caring, faithful and everything your ex was not. He is a dream. Or maybe you have glaring imperfections and never thought any man would even want to be with you but now here he is, showering you with love, and you feel like you can't afford to let anything stop this love. He too is a man of your dream.

What do you do when the man who loves you is your heart's desire and you love him back so deeply? You are drawn into a place where you would do just about anything for him because you love him. Sometimes you can get pulled into doing things because you want him to be happy and you want to keep him. Your need for his love and your own love for him are so strong that you don't want to lose him. This sounds like a love that should have no boundaries at all. We should be able to throw ourselves in and lose ourselves in it, shouldn't we? No! No! No! If there was ever a need for a boundary, this is probably the most important one. We can never be so beloved that we lose ourselves, abandon our principles, give up our goals or forsake our ideals. Yes, we all make some sacrifices for love. I never planned on having a child as a medical student but when I learned that having a child was a deep need of my husband's, I bit the bullet and we had a child. It cost me many sleepless nights at a time when I was working 60-80 hours a week. But when it is your fear of losing him that causes you to lose things of value to you, then you have crossed the most precious boundary of all and given up your own self-worth.

The "O" Factor Woman is so honored to be loved by the man of her dreams, but she is not so honored that she gives up on who she is. She knows her worth and values herself so much that she is not afraid to say "no" when the man of her dreams asks her to do something that is wrong. She is not ruled by fear; she is ruled by faith. She knows that the true man of her dreams will not take advantage of her. Instead he will spur her on to be a better person while she spurs him on to do the same.

What a wonderful feeling to be loved! One final thought on being the beloved. Who is this guy who loves you? What is his role in society? What is his career? What are his goals? What demands are placed on him by his family? He might love and adore you, but you might not be the only person/thing to which he is bound. Are you willing to share? Princess Kate had to agree to share Prince William with all of England. She also had to agree to be an international icon who would be chased by cameras for the rest of her life. She had to decide that this was okay with her in order for her to accept his love and be his beloved. Who loves you? Who is it that has made you the object of his affection? He might be okay, good, or the man of your dreams but before you accept his love, be sure that you are willing and able to share him. Be sure that you are up for the task of being his beloved. Be sure that you are willing and able to make the sacrifices while enjoying the benefits of being beloved. If you want to rock the beloved hat, then pay attention to the boundaries!

Hats off to these beloved women.

OUR EXAMPLE - Queen Vashti

Vashti was fine! She was so fine that her husband just liked to look at her. She was the beloved queen. Her husband King Ahasuerus was a bit of an icon himself. He threw a 6-month long party just to show off his kingdom! When that was over, he had a feast for all his officials and allowed them to drink whatever they wanted in whatever quantities they wanted. And when he was drunk with wine, he called for Vashti to be brought forth and paraded in front of the drunk King and his drunk officials. As beloved as Vashti was, she was not so loved that she allowed her lover to treat her anyhow. She is an example to us to refuse to be so beloved that we forget who we are.

OUR EXAMPLE – Bathsheba

One thing that sets a beloved woman apart as an example is when she doesn't just use the love and favor given to her for selfish gain.

David loved Bathsheba. My goodness that was one serious life changing rooftop bath she took! Before she knew it, she was caught up in a whirlwind of an affair, a murder and a rebuke from the prophet. But when that was all over, she had a son Solomon who was loved by David but most importantly was loved by God. In fact we don't hear much about Bathsheba after that, but when we do see her, she is using her beloved status for a good cause. Adonijah had made himself king and King David was too old to keep track of all the happenings in the kingdom. That's when Bathsheba stepped in to save the day, prompted by Prophet Nathan. Bathsheba used her beloved status to secure the throne for Solomon, a position that had already been determined by God. It feels so good to be loved; in fact it is pretty awesome. Let that love count for something good.

Watch out for these beloved women.

OUR CAUTION - Queen Vashti

Queen Vashti was our example because she didn't let the love stop her from standing up for herself but there is another lesson for us concerning how to handle being beloved. I don't know how Vashti became Queen. I don't know if she was forced or if she agreed. But once you become Queen, you are practically a slave to the King. The Queen was not allowed to reject the King in any way shape or form. Vashti's story is an example but it also a caution because we need to be clear about who we have allowed to love us. If you enjoy the gifts and showers of love so much that you agree to be the beloved of a rich drug dealer, then you have got to expect the guns and death that come with the role. Don't be so caught up in being beloved that you fail to see the big picture. Vashti did not understand the big picture of what it meant to be the beloved of the King. It meant that when he called you to come up and display yourself before him and his drunken friends, you had to obey or risk losing your life. It's nice to be beloved, but understand your obligation to that guy who loves you because being beloved is not free.

OUR CAUTION – Bathsheba

Make no mistake about it: Bathsheba had no business being in David's bed. Yes, this was a power struggle issue and truth be told we are not told what happened behind the scenes. Did Bathsheba say no to the king's advances? Was she a willing participant? Was she just so excited about being called to the palace that she forgot she was a married woman? We don't know all the details of how this happened, but her story is still a caution to us as women because we can be so caught up in being loved that we fail to take a stand for righteousness. Vashti took the risk to stand up for herself in a precarious situation where she had no legal right to disobey the king and she paid the price. In Bathsheba's case we don't know how she responded. Her stance is not made clear in scripture. When you are being loved in a situation that is wrong, let your response be clear:

No!

This woman wore the beloved hat in all the wrong ways

OUR WARNING – Hosea's Wife Gomer

Gomer married Hosea and had 3 children with him but she was just there for the ride. She had no intention of being a faithful wife. It didn't matter that Hosea loved her. After all God Himself had commanded Hosea to marry her. He loved her so much and would do anything for her. He even had to go and buy her back from some guy. Imagine that? Paying money to bring your own wife home? Yet Hosea loved her that much. But God had her brought in because He knew she would not stay faithful no matter how much Hosea loved her. Just like Israel, being beloved by a faithful man of God would not be enough. She would leave her true love and go chasing after love in all the wrong places. What a tragedy!

This woman had the "O" Factor!

She wore the beloved hat with BOUNDARIES

OUR GOAL – Hannah

Hannah was on the double portion love plan. When it came to being loved, Hannah was the definition of being beloved and her husband Elkanah had no problem letting it be known that he loved her. Her barrenness did not deter him; he still preferred her to his other wife with all the children. He loved her so much that he showered her with double portions, much more than she needed. Unfortunately her rival Penninah also took it upon herself to provoke Hannah and make her miserable, unhappy and anorexic year after year. Elkanah was so troubled by all of this that he tried to convince Hannah that his love was enough for her, and that she should be content because he was better than ten sons. Hmm. So Hannah had a choice (1) Be content with all this love but remain miserable (2) Enjoy the love, but still set your heart on purpose. Hannah put her boundaries in the right place. She chose option #2. She wanted a son, and she recognized that God needed a prophet so made a deal with God. The deal went like this, "Ok Lord, you see how terrible my life is. Yes Elkanah loves me like crazy and I like it but that woman is driving me crazy! The only thing that's gonna shut her up and stop my sorrow is if I have a child. Now I've been coming here year after year and in a couple of years, you are going to need a real priest up in this place. So if you have mercy on me and give me a son, I will give him back to you. What do you say?" God liked that plan. He gave Hannah a son, and He got Samuel, one of the most beloved prophets of Israel. Samuel would not have come into the world if Hannah was satisfied with her beloved status. Hannah didn't let love stop her from fulfilling destiny. She moved the boundary to where it needed to be: where she would have a son and still be beloved!

Do you have The "O" Factor?

Rate yourself on each of the principles. Use a scale of 1 (I do not have this at all) to 10 (I've got this one covered) Rate yourself on the principles needed even for the hats you may not wear now. "O" Factor women rock the principles with or without the hat!

Sister	WISDOM	1 2 3 4 5 6 7 8 9 10
Worker	BALANCE	1 2 3 4 5 6 7 8 9 10
Daughter	PRACTICE	1 2 3 4 5 6 7 8 9 10
Friend	SENSE	1 2 3 4 5 6 7 8 9 10
Wife	ENDURANCE	1 2 3 4 5 6 7 8 9 10
Rival	PERSPECTIVE	1 2 3 4 5 6 7 8 9 10
Mistress	STRENGTH	1 2 3 4 5 6 7 8 9 10
Servant	SELF-WORTH	1 2 3 4 5 6 7 8 9 10
Lover	TIMING	1 2 3 4 5 6 7 8 9 10
Mother	VISION	1 2 3 4 5 6 7 8 9 10
Rejected	PURPOSE	1 2 3 4 5 6 7 8 9 10
Beloved	BOUNDARIES	1 2 3 4 5 6 7 8 9 10

Total possible score: 120 (P.S. Even Wonder Woman can't score 120!)

Your score today: _____

Do you have The "O" Factor?

Study each of the principles you scored low on. Work on yourself in the next six months. Read the book again and this time, take notes for yourself! Be intentional about growing in each of the principles. And then score yourself again.

Sister	WISDOM	1	2	3	4	5	6	7	8	9	10
Worker	BALANCE	1	2	3	4	5	6	7	8	9	10
Daughter	PRACTICE	1	2	3	4	5	6	7	8	9	10
Friend	SENSE	1	2	3	4	5	6	7	8	9	10
Wife	ENDURANCE	1	2	3	4	5	6	7	8	9	10
Rival	PERSPECTIVE	1	2	3	4	5	6	7	8	9	10
Mistress	STRENGTH	1	2	3	4	5	6	7	8	9	10
Servant	SELF-WORTH	1	2	3	4	5	6	7	8	9	10
Lover	TIMING	1	2	3	4	5	6	7	8	9	10
Mother	VISION	1	2	3	4	5	6	7	8	9	10
Rejected	PURPOSE	1	2	3	4	5	6	7	8	9	10
Beloved	BOUNDARIES	1	2	3	4	5	6	7	8	9	10

Total possible score: 120 (P.S. Wonder Woman still can't score 120!)

Your score today: _____

The "O" Factor

Reference Sheet

Hat	Key	Biblical Reference	
Sister Hat Principle: WISDOM	Know who you are, know who your siblings are, have healthy expectations of them and have healthy expectations of yourself!	**Example:** Mary & Martha **Caution:** Leah & Rachel **Warning:** Lots' girls **Goal:** Zelophehad's daughters	John 11:1-46 Gen. 29 & 30 Gen. 19:30-38 Numbers 27
Worker Hat Principle: BALANCE	Make all your other hats work together! Without balance you will be miserable at work and everywhere else.	**Example:** Rizpah **Caution:** Martha **Warning:** Miriam **Goal:** Lydia	2 Sam. 21:8-14 Luke 10:38-42 Numbers 12 Acts 16:13-15
Daughter Hat Principle: PRACTICE	First be a daughter of God. When you know how to walk with God as your heavenly Father, you will be amazing as an earthly daughter!	**Example:** Miriam **Example:** Jepththah's daughter **Caution:** Herodias's daughter **Warning:** Athaliah **Goal:** Esther **Goal:** Rahab	Exodus 2:4-8 Judges 11 Mark 6:17-28 2 Chron. 22-24 Esther 2:10 Joshua 2
Friend Hat Principle: SENSE	Think before you act or react! Handle your friends just like you should handle your sisters: with sensible expectations!	**Example:** Naomi's friends **Caution:** Daughters of Jerusalem **Warning:** The Housemates **Warning:** Euodia & Synteche **Goal:** Jesus' posse	Ruth 1:20, 4:13-17 Song of Songs 5:9, 6:1 I Kings 3:16-28, Philippians 4:2-3 Luke 8:1-3

The "O" Factor

Reference Sheet

Hat	Key	Biblical Reference	
Wife Hat Principle: ENDURANCE	Be able to handle pressure. Being a wife is no easy task. You have to be prepared to do the work it takes to find the right husband, wait for the right time, and handle all the drama that the wife hat comes with! A wife needs endurance!	**Example:** Virtuous Woman **Example:** Abigail **Caution:** Job's Wife **Caution:** Sarai **Warning:** Jezebel **Warning:** Zaresh **Goal:** Priscilla **Goal:** Pilate's Wife	Proverbs 31 I Samuel 25 Job 2:9-10 Genesis 16 & 21 I Kings 21 Esther 5:14, 6:13 Acts 18 Matthew 27:19-24
Rival Hat Principle: PERSPECTIVE	Look at yourself in the mirror more times than you look at your rival. Keep a godly perspective	**Example:** Leah & Rachel **Caution:** Penninah **Warning:** Michal **Goal:** Shiphrah & Puah	Genesis 29 - 30 I Samuel 1 II Sam 6:16-23 Exodus 1:15-21
Mistress Hat Principle: STRENGTH	Be able to handle the pressure	**Example:** Eve **Caution:** Sarai **Warning:** Potiphar's wife **Goal:** Deborah	Genesis 2-4 Genesis 16 Genesis 39:7-20 Judges 4&5
Servant Hat Principle: SELF-WORTH	Know what you bring to the table. If you don't know who you are, you will despise the unique opportunities you have to serve others and the resulting blessings that will come to you.	**Example:** Naaman's servant **Caution:** Hagar **Warning:** Fortune Teller **Goal:** Ruth	I Kings 5 Genesis 16 Acts 16:16 Ruth

The "O" Factor

Reference Sheet

Hat	Key	Biblical Reference	
Lover Hat Principle: TIMING	Know when it's time to love and the right times to exhibit the various expressions of love to the people we love.	**Example:** Peter's wife **Caution:** Mary Magdalene **Warning:** Sapphira **Goal:** Beloved	I Cor 9:5 John 20 Acts 5 Song of Songs
Mother Hat Principle: VISION	See beyond now. Vision is the foundation of a mother's love.	**Example:** Naomi **Caution: Hagar** **Warning:** Herodias **Goal:** Jochebed	Ruth 3 Genesis 16 Mark 6:14-29 Exodus 2:1-10
Rejected Hat Principle: PURPOSE	Know your purpose and walk in it in spite of the rejection.	**Example:** Widow **Example:** Anna **Caution:** Tamar **Warning:** Potiphar's wife **Goal:** Tamar	Luke 18:1-6 Luke 2:36-38 II Samuel 13 Genesis 39:7-20 Genesis 38
Beloved Hat Principle: BOUNDARIES	Maintain necessary boundaries no matter how loved you are.	**Example:** Vashti & Bathsheba **Caution:** Vashti & Bathsheba **Warning:** Gomer **Goal:** Hannah	Esther 1, I Kings 1 Esther 1, IISamuel 11 Hosea 1 & 3 I Samuel 1:5-20

ABOUT THE AUTHOR

Dr. Sybil B. Pentsil is a multi-talented woman who wears many hats as she makes her impact on society. Not only is she a Doctor of Pediatric Academic medicine at the Sinai Hospital of Baltimore, she is also an ordained minister, serving as pastor at the House of Worship in Owings Mills, Maryland.

Sybil has written and co-authored many booklets and training guides for classes on premarital training, marriage counseling, spiritual development and leadership training. Her books include Free to Dance: Gaining Victory Over Your Thoughts and Emotions and Motherhood Redefined, both available from Better Life Today. In 2005, Sybil and her husband Fiifi co-founded Better Life Today, a self-improvement organization. They are known internationally for impacting marriages & businesses.

Sybil's youth was spent in various interesting parts of the world including New York, Ghana, and Liberia. She attended University at Albany in upstate New York and graduated summa cum laude with a degree in Chemistry. Afterward moving to Maryland to attend the world-renowned Johns Hopkins University School of Medicine and

Public Health. After completing residency training at Sinai Hospital in Baltimore in 2000, she received her medical degree and masters in public health respectively.

With this incredible background, it is no surprise that Sybil is a gifted teacher who addresses a broad variety of topics & teachings including personal leadership, training & development, time management, women & ministry, marriage, child development, parenting, pediatric care & management, and much more. Sybil speaks at conferences, seminars, youth groups, medical meetings, schools, churches, businesses, and other groups. She also conducts one-on-one counseling sessions.

Sybil and Fiifi are committed to family and enjoy traveling internationally with their children. They have three awesome sons – Jeremy, Jason, and Jesse.

Find more information about Dr. Pentsil:
Facebook: https://www.facebook.com/PastorSybil
Website: http://www.betterlife2day.org